THE MASS

The Massey Lectures are co-sponsored by CBC Radio, House of Anansi Press, and Massey College in the University of Toronto. The series was created in honour of the Right Honourable Vincent Massey, former Governor General of Canada, and was inaugurated in 1961 to provide a forum on radio where major contemporary thinkers could address important issues of our time.

This book comprises the 2008 Massey Lectures, "Payback," broadcast in November 2008 as part of CBC Radio's *Ideas* series. The producer of the series was Philip Coulter; the executive producer was Bernie Lucht.

MARGARET ATWOOD

Margaret Atwood is one of the world's pre-eminent writers — winner of the Booker Prize, the Scotiabank Giller Prize, the Governor General's Literary Award, the Franz Kafka International Literary Prize, the PEN Center USA Lifetime Achievement Award, the Premio Mondello in Italy, Le Chevalier dans l'Ordre des Arts et des Lettres in France, and the Prince of Asturias Prize for letters in Spain, among many other honours. She is the bestselling author of more than fifty books of poetry, fiction, and nonfiction, including *The Handmaid's Tale*, *Alias Grace*, *The Blind Assassin*, the MaddAddam Trilogy, *Hag-Seed*, and her most recent novel, *The Testaments*. She lives in Toronto and on Pelee Island in Lake Erie. She and her spouse, writer Graeme Gibson, are the Joint Honourary Presidents of the Rare Bird Club within Birdlife International. She is an International Vice President of PEN.

FICTION

The Edible Woman (1969)
Surfacing (1972)
Lady Oracle (1976)
Dancing Girls (1977)
Life Before Man (1979)
Bodily Harm (1981)
Murder in the Dark (1983)
Bluebeard's Egg (1983)
The Handmaid's Tale (1985)
Cat's Eye (1988)
Wilderness Tips (1991)
Good Bones (1992)
The Robber Bride (1993)
Good Bones and Simple Murders (1994)
Alias Grace (1996)
The Blind Assassin (2000)
Oryx and Crake (2003)
The Penelopiad (2005)
The Tent (2006)
Moral Disorder (2006)
The Year of the Flood (2009)
MaddAddam (2013)
Stone Mattress (2014)
Angel Catbird (2016–2018)
Hag-Seed (2016)
The Testaments (2019)

NONFICTION

Survival: A Thematic Guide to Canadian Literature (1972)
Days of the Rebels 1815–1840 (1977)
Second Words: Selected Critical Prose 1960–1982 (1982)
Strange Things: The Malevolent North in Canadian Literature (1996)
Negotiating with the Dead: A Writer on Writing (2002)

Moving Targets: Writing with Intent 1982–2004 (2004)
Writing with Intent: Essays, Reviews, Personal Prose 1983–2005 (2005)
In Other Worlds: SF and the Human Imagination (2011)

POETRY

The Circle Game (1965)
The Animals in That Country (1968)
The Journals of Susanna Moodie (1970)
Procedures for Underground (1970)
Power Politics (1971)
You Are Happy (1974)
Selected Poems (1976)
Two-Headed Poems (1978)
True Stories (1981)
Interlunar (1984)
Morning in the Burned House (1996)
Eating Fire: Selected Poems 1965–1995 (1998)
The Door (2007)

FOR CHILDREN

Up in the Tree (1978)
Anna's Pet [with Joyce C. Barkhouse] (1980)
For the Birds (1990)
Princess Prunella and the Purple Peanut (1995)
Rude Ramsay and the Roaring Radishes (2003)
Bashful Bob and Doleful Dorinda (2004)
Wandering Wenda and Widow Wallop's Wunderground Washery (2011)
A Trio of Tolerable Tales (2017)

PAYBACK

....

Debt and the Shadow Side of Wealth

MARGARET ATWOOD

First published in Canada in 2008 and the USA in 2008 by House of Anansi Press Inc.
This edition published in Canada in 2019 and the USA in 2019 by
House of Anansi Press Inc.
www.houseofanansi.com

CBC and Massey College logos used with permission.

House of Anansi Press is committed to protecting our natural environment.
As part of our efforts, this book is made of material from well-managed
FSC®-certified forests, recycled materials, and other controlled sources.

23 22 21 20 19   1 2 3 4 5

Library and Archives Canada Cataloguing in Publication

Title: Payback : debt and the shadow side of wealth / Margaret Atwood.
Names: Atwood, Margaret, 1939– author.
Description: Includes bibliographical references and index.
Identifiers: Canadiana 20190056444 | ISBN 9781487006976 (softcover)
Subjects: LCSH: Debt—Social aspects. | LCSH: Debt in literature.
Classification: LCC PS8501.T86 P39 2019 | DDC C814/.54—dc23

Library of Congress Control Number: 2019931303

Cover design: Bill Douglas
Text design and typesetting: Ingrid Paulson

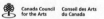

*We acknowledge for their financial support of our publishing program the Canada
Council for the Arts, the Ontario Arts Council, and the Government of Canada.*

Printed and bound in Canada

For Graeme and Jess,
and Matthew and Graeme the younger

(CONTENTS)

(INTRODUCTION TO THE 2019 EDITION)

ALTHOUGH MY MASSEY LECTURES, collectively titled *Payback: Debt and the Shadow Side of Wealth*, were greeted as prophetic when they first appeared in the fall of 2008, I did not foresee the writing of them. So much for my prophetic powers. But here is how I came by that undeserved reputation, in this instance.

By the early 2000s, I'd spent some years dodging various invitations to give the prestigious CBC Massey Lectures, which were inaugurated in 1961 to provide a forum on radio where "major contemporary thinkers could address important issues of our time." Those lectures are a lot of work! First you must write the lectures. Then you must turn the lectures into a book, which must be somewhat longer than the lectures themselves. Then you must deliver the lectures, one after another, in five different widely spaced cities across Canada, pausing only long enough to put on and remove your long underwear, as fall weather can be variable. Finally you must edit the lectures down to size for the radio broadcast.

This inflating and depuffing routine poses challenges, not only to one's skills but to one's ego — if the lectures should now be made shorter, having previously been made longer, how much faith can you place in the infallibility of each of your golden words?

So every time I was asked to deliver the Massey Lectures, I politely declined. "Thanks very much, but I'll be washing my hair," I said in effect. "And I'll be washing it next year too, and also the year after that, and..." Here I must explain the metaphor. It's from the 1950s, and it was what you were supposed to say in order to sidestep a date you didn't want to go on.

And so time passed — a time when I was always washing my hair when the subject of my delivering the Massey Lectures came up. But then Fate intervened. The Massey Lectures had traditionally been published by House of Anansi Press, a small literary company I'd kicked some founding money into back in the 1960s, whose board I'd subsequently served on while editing some of its books, and for which I'd written a tome called *Survival*, as part of the ongoing effort to prop up its finances. Anansi is now a mid-sized and very respectable press, but in 2002, it was in dire straits. It had been bought by a larger Canadian publisher, Stoddart, a while earlier, but now Stoddart itself was about to go down the drain, and Anansi would be gurgling into oblivion along with it.

In the nick of time, a man named Scott Griffin — who'd needed to be pried out of his Superman costume when a child — swooped in and bought Anansi, plucking it from the Slough of Despond, carrying its limp form to the shore, and restoring its breath of life with a judicious injection of cold cash. But meanwhile the Massey Lectures invitational circle had prudently decided to remove the lecture series from Anansi and bestow it on a larger and more solvent company.

Many were the wailings and dismal were the dirges! Couldn't I *do* something? A wart-removing potion, a curse or charm, an invocation to the moon? Something with an asp? I did not then and do not now have super-natural powers, but I gave it my best shot. I sat down and composed a zinger, in my best Anne of Green Gables tantrum mode, to this effect:

If you take the Masseys away from House of Anansi, I will never, never, never give the Massey Lectures, ever! (Stomp of foot.)

They didn't take the Masseys away from Anansi. Probably nothing to do with me, but you can see what would of necessity follow. And it did.

Expletive! I exclaimed. *Now I have to actually give the (expletive deleted) Massey Lectures!*

It was a fine example of the theme I was shortly to find myself exploring: on the face of it, they had done me a favour. I owed them. I had to repay them.

So I said I would give the Massey Lectures, without knowing what I would give them about. I fidgeted, I pro-crastinated, I pondered, weak and weary, over many a quaint and curious volume of forgotten lore.

Eventually I found myself circling around a set of questions that were bound to occur to anyone who had studied the nineteenth-century authors at any length. Heathcliff goes away poor and comes back rich: how? (Not in any good way, we'll be bound.) Will Chad Newsome of *The Ambassadors* leave his accomplished and refined French mistress and return to manage the vulgar but profitable family business in New England? (We guess yes.) Would Madame Bovary have got away with adultery if she'd been better at double-entry bookkeeping and had not run into debt? (Without question, say we.) Every nineteenth-century novel you crack open may delude you at first with tales of love and romance, but at the core of each one lies a bank account. Or the lack of one.

When I announced to the expectant Massey board that I had chosen my topic and it was Debt, I am told they blenched and huddled.

They thought I was going to write about Economics. They were much relieved when I explained that, no, my subject was simply the way human beings have thought about what is owed, who owes it, and how it should be repaid — the balancing of the scales, in religion, literature, the criminal underworld, the revenge tragedy, and in Nature, an area in which we have, alas, vastly overdrawn our account.

The invitational committee wiped the beads of perspiration from their brows, and I submitted an outline and vanished down the rabbit hole of research. There was plenty of time. It was only 2007, and the lectures weren't due to be delivered until the fall of 2009.

Then Fate struck again. At the beginning 2008, the Massey folk came to me in the guise of supplicants. Their 2008 lecturer would not be ready in time, so could I *please, please, please* deliver my own lectures a year early?

It was February. I would have to have the text of the book done by June, so it could be published in time for October, when the lecture tour would start. It was a tall order.

"Give me a couple of researchers," I said, rolling up my sleeves. What are sleeves for if you can't roll them up?

Five months and many hours of keyboard-pounding later, we were sort of ready. Yet more perspiration was wiped from brows.

Then Fate struck a third time. Just as the book was published and the lecture tour began — in Newfoundland, as it happened — the Big Financial Meltdown and Crisis occurred. And mine was the only book out there that was — on the face of it — about this topic. "How did you know?" asked various admiring hedge-fund managers. Useless to reply that I hadn't known: there was the evidence, laid out in the form of the book you may or may not be about to read.

I do not have a crystal ball. If I really could predict the future, I'd have cornered the stock market long ago.

But anyone can make educated guesses. Some of mine are contained within these pages. The most important guess has to do with the fact that we are using up our natural savings at a much greater rate than we can currently replace them. Unless a lot of people wrench their heads out of the sand and stuff them into their thinking caps very soon, we are almost certainly going to be facing the bad future that is being experienced by my update of Scrooge in this book. But, true to the spirit of Dickens — who knows more about debt than most — I also provide a good future. It too is within our grasp. Will we as a species balance the environmental scales? Will we let ourselves off the hook? Will we bail ourselves out of Debtor's Prison?

Let's hope.

(ONE)

ANCIENT BALANCES

CANADIAN NATURE WRITER Ernest Thompson Seton had an odd bill presented to him on his twenty-first birthday. It was a record kept by his father of all the expenses connected with young Ernest's childhood and youth, including the fee charged by the doctor for delivering him. Even more oddly, Ernest is said to have paid it. I used to think that Mr. Seton Senior was a jerk, but now I'm wondering, What if he was — in principle — right? Are we in debt to anyone or anything for the bare fact of our existence? If so, what do we owe, and to whom or to what? And how should we pay?

THE MOTIVE FOR this book is curiosity — mine — and my hope is that the writing of it will allow me to explore a subject I know little about, but which for this reason intrigues me. That subject is debt.

   Payback is not about debt management, or sleep debt, or the national debt, or about managing your monthly budget, or about how debt is actually a good thing because you can borrow money and then make it grow, or about shopaholics and how to figure out that you are one: bookstores and the Internet abound in such materials.

Nor is it about more lurid forms of debt: gambling debts and Mafia revenges, karmic justice whereby bad deeds trigger reincarnation as a beetle, or melodramas in which moustache-twirling creditors use nonpayment of the rent to force unwanted sex on beautiful women, though it may touch on these. Instead, it's about debt as a human construct — thus an imaginative construct — and how this construct mirrors and magnifies both voracious human desire and ferocious human fear.

Writers write about what worries them, says Alistair MacLeod. Also about what puzzles them, I'd add. The subject of *Payback* is one of the most worrisome and puzzling things I know: that peculiar nexus where money, narrative or story, and religious belief intersect, often with explosive force.

THE THINGS THAT puzzle us as adults begin by puzzling us as children, or this has certainly been the case for me. In the late 1940s society in which I grew up, there were three things you were never supposed to ask questions about. One of them was money, especially how much of it anyone made. The second was religion: to begin a conversation on that subject would lead directly to the Spanish Inquisition, or worse. The third was sex. I lived among the biologists, and sex — at least as practised by insects — was something I could look up in the textbooks that were lying around the house: the ovipositor was no stranger to me. So the burning curiosity children experience vis-à-vis the forbidden was focused, for me, on the two other taboo areas: the financial and the devotional.

At first these appeared to be distinct categories. There were the things of God, which were unseen. Then there were the things of Caesar, which were all too material. They took the form of golden calves, of which we didn't have many in Toronto at that time, and also the form of money, the love of which was the root of all evil. But on the other hand stood the comic-book character Scrooge McDuck — much read about by me — who was a hot-tempered, tight-fisted, and often devious billionaire named after Charles Dickens's famous redeemed miser, Ebenezer Scrooge. The plutocratic McDuck had a large money bin full of gold coins, in which he and his three adopted nephews splashed around as if in a swimming pool. Money, for Uncle Scrooge and the young duck trip-lets, was not the root of all evil but a pleasurable plaything. Which of these views was correct?

We kids of the 1940s did usually have some pocket money, and although we weren't supposed to talk about it or have an undue love of it, we were expected to learn to manage it at an early age. When I was eight years old, I had my first paying job. I was already acquainted with money in a more limited way — I got five cents a week as an allowance, which bought a lot more tooth decay then than it does now. The pennies not spent on candy I kept in a tin box that had once held Lipton tea. It had a brightly coloured Indian design, complete with elephant, opulent veiled lady, men in turbans, temples and domes, palm trees, and a sky so blue it never was. The pennies had leaves on one side and king's heads on the other, and were desirable to me according to their rarity and beauty: King George the Sixth, the reigning monarch, was common currency and thus low-ranking on my snobby little scale, and also he had no beard or moustache; but there were still some hairier George the Fifths in circulation, and, if you were lucky, a really fur-faced Edward the Seventh or two.

I understood that these pennies could be traded for goods such as ice cream cones, but I did not think them superior to the other units of currency used by my fellow children: cigarette-package airplane cards, milk-bottle tops, comic books, and glass marbles of many kinds. Within each of these categories, the principle was the same: rarity and beauty increased value. The rate of exchange was set by the children themselves, though a good deal of haggling took place.

All of that changed when I got a job. The job paid twenty-five cents an hour — a fortune! — and consisted of wheeling a baby around in the snow. As long as I brought the baby back, alive and not too frozen, I got the twenty-five cents. It was at this time in my life that each penny came to be worth the same as every other penny, despite whose head was on it, thus teaching me an important lesson: in high finance, aesthetic considerations soon drop by the wayside, worse luck.

Since I was making so much money, I was told I needed a bank account, so I graduated from the Lipton tea tin and acquired a red bank book. Now the difference between the pennies with heads on them and the marbles, milk-bottle tops, comic books, and airplane cards became clear, because you could not put the marbles into the bank. But you were urged to put your money in there, in order to keep it safe. When I'd accumulated a dangerous amount of the stuff — say, a dollar — I would deposit it at the bank, where the sum was recorded in pen and ink by an intimidating bank teller. The last number in the series was called "the balance" — not a term I understood, as I had yet to see a two-armed weighing scales.

Every once in a while an extra sum would appear in my red bank book — one I hadn't deposited. This, I was told, was called "interest," and I had "earned" it by having kept my money in the bank. I didn't understand this either. It was certainly interesting to me that I had some extra money — that must be why it was called "interest" — but I knew I hadn't actually earned it: no babies from the bank had been wheeled around in the snow by me. Where then had these mysterious sums come from? Surely from the same imaginary place that spawned the nickels left by the Tooth Fairy in exchange for your shucked-off teeth: some realm of pious invention that couldn't be located anywhere exactly, but that we all had to pretend to believe in or the tooth-for-a-nickel gambit would no longer work.

However, the nickels under the pillow were real enough. So was the bank interest, because you could cash it in and turn it back into pennies, and thence into candy and ice cream cones. But how could a fiction generate real objects? I knew from fairy tales such as *Peter Pan* that if you ceased to believe in fairies they would drop dead: if I stopped believing in banks, would they too expire? The adult view was that fairies were unreal and banks were real. But was that true?

Thus began my financial puzzlements. Nor are they over yet.

DURING THE PAST half-century I've spent much time riding around on public transport. I always read the ads. In the 1950s, there were a lot of girdle and brassiere ads, and ads for deodorants and mouthwashes. Today these have vanished, to be replaced by ads for diseases — heart problems, arthritis, diabetes, and more; ads to help you stop smoking; ads for television series that always feature a goddesslike woman or two, though these are sometimes ads for hair dye and skin cream; and ads for agencies you can call if you have a gambling addiction. And ads for debt services — there are a lot of this kind.

One of them shows a gleefully smiling woman with a young child. The caption says, "Now I'm in charge... and the collection calls have stopped." "Like hell money doesn't buy happiness — debt is manageable," says another.

"There *is* Life after Debt!" punningly chirps a third. "There *can* be a happily ever after part!" trills a fourth, catering to the same belief in fairy tales that inspired you to shove the bills under the rug and then make believe they'd been paid. "Is someone on your tail?" queries a fifth ad, more ominously, from the back end of a bus. These services promise, not to make your burdensome debts vanish in a puff of smoke, but to help you to consolidate them and pay them down in bits and pieces, while learning to avoid the free-spending behaviour that got you so deeply into the red in the first place.

Why are there so many of these ads? Is it because there are unprecedented numbers of people in debt? Very possibly.

In the 1950s, the age of girdles and deodorants, the adsters evidently felt that the most anxiety-making thing imaginable was to have your body lolloping about unconfined, and stinking up the place into the bargain. It was the body that might get away from you, so it was the body that had to be brought under control; if not, that body might get out and do things that would bring a shame upon you so deep and sexual that it could never be mentioned on public transport. Now things are very different. Sexual antics are a part of the entertainment industry, and thus no longer a matter for censure and guilt, so your body is not the main focus of anxiety unless it gets one of the much-advertised diseases. Instead, the worrisome thing is the debit side of your ledger.

There's good reason for this. The first credit card was introduced in 1950. In 1955, the average Canadian household debt-to-income ratio was 55 percent; in 2003, it was 105.2 percent. The ratio has gone up since then. In the United States the ratio was 114 percent in 2004. In other words, a great many people are spending more than they're earning. So are a great many national governments.

On the microeconomic level, a friend tells me of an epidemic of debt among over-eighteens, especially college students: credit card companies target them, and the students rush out and spend the maximum without stopping to calculate the consequences and are then stuck with debts they can't pay off, at very high interest rates. Since neurologists are now telling us that the adolescent brain is quite different from the adult one, and not really capable of doing the long-term buy-now, pay-later math, this ought to be considered child exploitation.

At the other end of the scale, the financial world has recently been shaken as a result of the collapse of a debt pyramid involving something called "sub-prime mortgages"— a pyramid scheme that most people don't grasp very well, but that boils down to the fact that some large financial institutions peddled mortgages to people who could not possibly pay the monthly rates and then put this snake-oil debt into cardboard boxes with impressive labels on them and sold them to institutions and hedge funds that thought they were worth something. It's like the teenage credit card ploy, but at a much greater level of magnitude.

A friend of mine from the United States writes: "I used to have three banks and a mortgage company. Bank One bought the other two and is now trying hard to buy the mortgage company, which is bankrupt, only it was revealed this morning that the last bank standing is also in serious trouble. Now they are trying to renegotiate with the mortgage company. Question One: If your company is going broke, why would you want to buy a company whose insolvency is front-page news? Question Two: If all the lenders go broke, will the borrowers get off the hook? You can't imagine the chagrin of the credit-loving American. I gather that whole neighbourhoods in the Midwest look like neighbourhoods in my hometown, empty houses with knee-high grass and vines growing over them and no one willing to admit they actually own the place. Down we go, about to reap what we sow."

Which has a nice Biblical ring to it, but still we scratch our heads. How and why did this happen? The answer I hear quite often —"greed"— may be accurate enough, but it doesn't go very far toward unveiling the deeper mysteries of the process. What is this "debt" by which we're so bedevilled? Like air, it's all around us, but we never think about it unless something goes wrong with the supply. Certainly it's a thing we've come to feel is indispensable to our collective buoyancy. In good times we float around on it as if on a helium-filled balloon; we rise higher and higher, and the balloon gets bigger and bigger, until — *poof!* — some killjoy sticks a pin into it and we sink. But what is the nature of that pin? Another friend of mine used to maintain that airplanes stayed up in the air only because people believed — against reason — that they could fly: without that collective delusion sustaining them, they would instantly plummet to earth. Is "debt" similar?

In other words, perhaps debt exists because we imagine it. It is the forms this imagining has taken — and their impact on lived reality — that I would like to explore.

OUR PRESENT ATTITUDES toward debt are deeply embedded in our entire culture — culture being, as primatologist Frans de Waal has said, "an extremely powerful modifier — affecting everything we do and are, penetrating to the core of human existence." But perhaps there are some even more basic patterns being modified.

Let's assume that all of the things human beings do — the good, the bad, and the ugly — can be located on a smorgasbord of behaviours with a sign on it reading *Homo sapiens sapiens*. These things aren't on the smorgasbord labelled *Spiders*, which is why we don't spend a lot of time eating bluebottle flies, nor are they on the smorgasbord labelled *Dogs*, which is why we don't go around marking fire hydrants with our glandular scents or shoving our noses into bags of old garbage. Part of our human smorgasbord has actual food on it, for, like all species, we are driven by appetite and hunger. The rest of the dishes on the table contain less concrete fears and desires — things such as "I'd like to fly," "I'd like to have sexual intercourse with you," "War is unifying to the tribe," "I'm afraid of snakes," and "What happens to me when I die?"

But there's nothing on the table that isn't based on or linked to our rudimentary human patterns — what we want, what we don't want, what we admire, what we despise, what we love, and what we hate and fear. Some geneticists even go so far as to speak of our "modules," as if we were electronic systems with chunks of functional circuitry that can be switched on and off. Whether such discrete modules actually exist as part of our genetically determined neural wiring is at present still a matter for experiment and debate. But in any case, I'm assuming that the older a recognizable pattern of behaviour is — the longer it's demonstrably been with us — the more integral it must be to our human-ness and the more cultural variations on it will be in evidence.

I'm not proposing a stamped-in-tin immutable "human nature" here — epigeneticists point out that genes can be expressed, or "switched on," and also suppressed in various ways, depending on the environment in which they find themselves. I'm merely saying that without gene-linked configurations — certain building blocks or foundation stones, if you like — the many variations of basic human behaviours that we see around us would never occur at all. An online video game such as *Everquest*, in which you have to work your way up from rabbit-skinner to castle-owning knight by selling and trading, co-operating with fellow players on group missions, and launching raids on other castles, would be unthinkable if we were not both a social species and one aware of hierarchies.

What corresponding ancient inner foundation stone underlies the elaborate fretwork of debt that surrounds us on every side? Why are we so open to offers of present-time advantage in exchange for future though onerous repayment? Is it simply that we're programmed to snatch the low-hanging fruit and gobble down as much of it as we can, without thinking ahead to the fruitless days that may then lie ahead of us? Well, partly: seventy-two hours without fluids or two weeks without food and you're most likely dead, so if you don't eat some of that low-hanging fruit right now you aren't going to be around six months later to congratulate yourself on your capacity for self-restraint and delayed gratification. In that respect, credit cards are almost guaranteed to make money for the lender, since "grab it now" may be a variant of a behaviour selected for in hunter-gatherer days, long before anyone ever thought about saving up for their retirement. A bird in the hand really was worth two in the bush then, and a bird crammed into your mouth was worth even more. But is it just a case of short-term gain followed by long-term pain? Is debt created from our own greed or even — more charitably — from our own need?

I postulate that there's another ancient inner foundation stone without which debt and credit structures could not exist: our sense of fairness. Viewed in the best light, this is an admirable human characteristic. Without our sense of fairness, the bright side of which is "one good turn deserves another," we wouldn't recognize the fairness of paying back what we've borrowed, and thus no one would ever be stupid enough to lend anything to anyone else with an expectation of return. Spiders don't share out the bluebottles among other adult spiders: only social animals indulge in sharing out. The dark side of the sense of fairness is the sense of unfairness, which results in gloating when you've got away with being unfair, or else guilt; and in rage and vengeance, when the unfairness has been visited upon you.

Children start saying, "That's not fair!" at the age of four or so, long before they're interested in sophisticated investment vehicles or have any sense of the value of coins and bills. They are also filled with satisfaction when the villain in a bedtime story gets an unambiguous comeuppance, and made uneasy when such retribution doesn't happen. Forgiveness and mercy, like olives and anchovies, seem to be acquired later, or — if the culture is unfavourable to them — not. But for young children, putting a bad person into a barrel studded with nails and rolling him or her into the sea restores the cosmic balance and removes the malevolent force from view, and the little ones sleep easier at night.

The interest in fairness elaborates with age. After seven, there's a legalistic phase in which the fairness — or, usually, the unfairness — of any rule imposed by adults is argued relentlessly. As this age, too, the sense of fairness can take curious forms. For instance, in the 1980s there was a strange ritual among nine-year-old children that went like this: during car rides, you stared out the window until you spotted a Volkswagen Beetle. Then you hit your child companion on the arm, shouting, "Punch-buggy, no punch-backs!" Seeing the Volkswagen Beetle first meant that you had the right to punch the other child, and adding a codicil—"No punch-backs!"—meant that he or she had been done out of the right to punch you in return. If, however, the other child managed to shout "Punch-backs!" before you could yell out your protective charm, then a retaliatory punch was in order. Money was not a factor here: you couldn't buy your way out of being punched. What was at issue was the principle of reciprocity: one punch deserved another, and would certainly get it unless an Out clause was inserted with the speed of lightning.

Ontogeny repeats phylogeny, we're told: the growth of the individual mirrors the developmental history of the species. Those who fail to discern in the Punch-buggy ritual the essential lex talionis form of the almost four-thousand-year-old Code of Hammurabi—reformulated as the Biblical eye-for-an-eye and tooth-for-a-tooth law—are blind indeed. Lex talionis means, roughly, "the law of retribution in kind or suitability." Under the Punch-buggy rules, punches cancel each other out unless you can whip your magical protection into place first. This kind of protection can be found throughout the world of contracts and legal documents, in clauses that begin with phrases such as "Notwithstanding any of the foregoing."

We'd all like the right to a free punch, or a free lunch, or a free anything. We all suspect that the likeliness of our getting such a right is scant unless we can jump in there with some serious abracadabra. But how do we know that one punch is likely to incur another? Is it early socialization — the kind you get while squabbling over the Play-Doh at preschool and then saying, "Melanie bit me"— or is it a template hot-wired into the human brain?

LET'S EXAMINE THE case for the latter. In order for a mental construct such as "debt" to exist — you owe me something that will balance the books once it is transferred to me — there are some preconditions. One of them, as I've said, is the notion of fairness. Attached to that is the notion of equivalent values: what does it take to make both sides of the mental score sheet or grudge tally or double-entry bookkeeping program we're all constantly running add up to the same thing? If Johnny has three apples and Suzie has a pencil, is one apple for one pencil an acceptable exchange, or will there be an apple or a pencil remaining to be paid? That all depends on what values Johnny and Suzie place on their respective trading items, which in turn depend on how hungry and/or in need of communication devices they may be. In a trade perceived as fair, each side balances the other, and nothing is thought to be owing.

Even inorganic Nature strives toward balances, otherwise known as static states. As a child, you may have done that elementary experiment in which you put salty water on one side of a permeable membrane and fresh water on the other side and measure how long it takes for the sodium chloride to make its way into the H_2O until both sides are equally salty. Or, as an adult, you may simply have noticed that if you put your cold feet on your partner's warm leg, your feet will get warmer while your partner's leg will get colder. (If you try this at home, please don't say I told you to do it.)

Many animals are able to tell "bigger than" apart from "smaller than." Hunting animals have to be able to do this, as it could be fatal to them to literally bite off more than they can chew. Eagles on the Pacific coast can be dragged to a watery grave by salmon that are too heavy for them, since, once having pounced, they can't unhook their claws unless they're on a firm surface. If you've ever taken small children to the big-cat enclosure at the zoo, you may have noticed that a medium-sized feline such as the cheetah won't pay much attention to you but will eye the kids with avid speculation, because the youngsters are meal-sized for them and you are not.

The ability to size up an enemy or a prey is a common feature of the animal kingdom, but among the primates, the making of fine bigger-than and better-than distinctions when the edible goodies are being divided up verges on the unnerving. In 2003, *Nature* magazine published an account of experiments conducted by Frans de Waal, of Emory University's Yerkes National Primate Center, and anthropologist Sarah F. Brosnan. To begin with, they taught capuchin monkeys to trade pebbles for slices of

cucumber. Then they gave one of the monkeys a grape —
viewed by the monkeys as more valuable — for the very
same pebble. "You can do it twenty-five times in a row,
and they are perfectly happy getting cucumber slices,"
said de Waal. But if a grape was substituted — thus
unfairly giving one monkey a better pay packet for work
of equal value — the cucumber-receivers got upset, began
throwing pebbles out of the cage, and eventually refused
to co-operate. And the majority of the monkeys got so
angry if one of them was given a grape for no reason that
some of them stopped eating. It was a monkey picket line:
they might as well have been carrying signs that read,
Management Grape Dispensing Unfair! The trading was
taught, as was the pebble/cucumber rate of exchange, but
the outrage appeared to be spontaneous.

Keith Chen, a researcher at the Yale School of Management, also worked with capuchin monkeys. He found he
could train them to use coinlike metal disks as currency,
coins being the pebble idea, only shiny. "My underlying
goal is to determine what aspects of our economic behaviour are innate, deep in the brain, and conserved over
time," said Chen. But why stop at obviously economic
behaviour such as trading? Among social animals that
need to co-operate in order to achieve common goals such
as — for capuchins — killing and eating squirrels, and —
for chimpanzees — killing and eating bush babies, there
has to be a sharing-out of the results of group effort that
is recognized as fair by the sharers. Fair is not the same
as equal: for instance, would it be fair for the plate of a

ninety-pound ten-year-old to contain exactly the same amount of food as that of a two-hundred-pound six-foot-sixer? Among the hunting chimpanzees, the one strongest in personality or physique typically gets more, but all who have joined in the hunt receive at least something, which is pretty much the same principle used by Genghis Khan for doling out the results of his conquering, slaughtering, and looting activities among his allies and troops. Those who express surprise at winning political parties for their porkbarrelling and favouritism might keep this in mind: if you don't share out, those folks won't be there when you need them. At the very least, you have to give them some cucumber slices, and avoid giving grapes to their rivals.

If fairness is completely lacking, the members of the chimpanzee group will rebel; at the very least, they're unlikely to join in a group hunt next time. To the extent that they're social animals interacting in complex communities in which status is important, primates are highly conscious of what's fitting for each member and what, on the other hand, constitutes uppity counter-jumping. The snobbish top-of-the-pecking-order Lady Catherine de Bourgh of Jane Austen's novel *Pride and Prejudice*, with her exquisitely calibrated sense of rank, has nothing on capuchin monkeys and chimpanzees.

Chimpanzees don't limit their trading to food; they regularly engage in mutually beneficial favour-trading, or reciprocal altruism. Chimp A helps Chimp B to gang

up on Chimp C and expects to be helped in turn. If Chimp
B then doesn't come through at the time of Chimp A's
need, Chimp A is enraged and throws a screaming tem-
per tantrum. There seems to be a kind of inner ledger
involved: Chimp A senses perfectly well what Chimp B
owes him, and Chimp B senses it too. Debts of honour
exist among chimpanzees, it appears. It's the same mechanism that's at work in Francis Ford Coppola's film *The
Godfather*: a man whose daughter has been disfigured
comes to the Mafia boss for help and gets it, but it's
understood that this favour will need to be repaid later in
some unsavoury way.

As Robert Wright says in his 1995 book, *The Moral
Animal: Why We Are the Way We Are*, "Reciprocal altruism has presumably shaped the texture not just of human
emotion, but of human cognition. Leda Cosmides has
shown that people are good at solving otherwise baffling
logical puzzles when the puzzles are cast in the form of
social exchange — in particular, when the object of the
game is to figure out if someone is cheating. This suggests to Cosmides that a 'cheater-detection' module is
among the mental organs governing reciprocal altruism.
No doubt others remain to be discovered." We do want
our trades and exchanges to be fair and above-board, at
least on the other person's side. A "cheater-detection
module" assumes a parallel module, one that evaluates
non-cheating. Small children used to chant, "Cheaters
never prosper!" in the schoolyard. That's true — we judge

cheaters harshly, which affects their future prosperity —
but it's also true, alas, that they receive this judgement
from us only when they get caught.

In *The Moral Animal*, Wright gives an account of a
computer simulation program that won a 1970s contest
proposed by Robert Axelrod, an American political sci-
entist. The contest was designed to test what sort of
behaviour patterns would prove to be the fittest by sur-
viving the longest in a series of encounters with other
programs. When one program first "met" another, it had
to decide whether to co-operate, whether to respond with
aggression or cheating, or whether to refuse to play. "The
context for the competition," says Wright, "nicely mir-
rored the social context of human, and prehuman
evolution. There was a fairly small society — several
dozen regularly interacting individuals. Each program
could 'remember' whether each other program had coop-
erated on previous encounters, and adjust its own
behaviour accordingly."

The winner of the contest was called TIT FOR TAT — an
expression that descends from "Tip for Tap," both words
having once meant a hit, push, or blow — thus, "You hit
me and I'll hit you back." The computer program TIT FOR
TAT played by a very simple set of rules: "On the first
encounter with any program, it would co-operate. There-
after, it would do whatever the other program had done
on a previous encounter. One good turn deserves another,
as does one bad turn." This program won out over time
because it was never repeatedly victimized — if an

opponent cheated on it, it withheld co-operation next time — and, unlike consistent cheaters and exploiters, it didn't alienate a lot of others and then find itself shut out of play, nor did it get involved in escalating aggression. It played by a recognizable eye-for-an-eye rule: Do unto others as they do unto you. (Which is not the same as the "golden rule"— Do unto others as you would have them do unto you. That one is much more difficult to follow.)

In the computer program contest won by TIT FOR TAT, it was a given that each player had equal resources at its disposal. Treating a first approach with friendliness and then replying to subsequent ones in kind — returning good for good and evil for evil — can be the winning stratagem only if the playing field is level. None of the competing programs were permitted to have superior weapons systems: had one of the entrants been allowed an advantage such as the chariot, the double-recurved bow of Genghis Khan, or the atomic bomb, TIT FOR TAT would have failed, because the player with the technological advantage could have obliterated its opponents, enslaved them, or forced them to trade on disadvantageous terms. This is in fact what has happened over the long course of our history: those that won the wars wrote the laws, and the laws they wrote enshrined inequality by justifying hierarchical social formations with themselves at the top.

I ENCOUNTERED THE "kind but stern" tit-for-tat pattern as a child, but in a literary guise. In Charles Kingsley's 1863 children's book, *The Water Babies*, Tom — a poor, ignorant, exploited, and abused child-labourer chimney sweep — drowns in a river and finds himself swimming around with gills, like a newt. Then, in a series of post-mortem adventures, he learns through trial and error how to become Kingsley's version of the ideal Victorian Christian male. His main instructors are two powerful supernatural female figures — the beautiful, baby-cuddling Mrs. Doasyouwouldbedoneby, who's the Golden Rule in action, and the ugly, strict, punitive but fair Mrs. Bedoneby-asyoudid, a nannyish embodiment of payback. The Victorian reader might have recognized them as Mercy and Justice, or even as a nurturing Wordsworthian Mother Nature — she "who never did betray the heart that loves her" — and a tough, take-no-prisoners Darwinian Mother Nature with a Lamarckian twist — you become what you do. (Kingsley was a friend of Darwin; *The Water Babies* was published a mere four years after *The Origin of Species* had appeared and is one of the first literary responses to it. It may even be counted as one of the first brave entries in the Intelligent Design category: if the Garden of Eden and Noah's Flood had to be scratched, at least you might fall back on Mrs. Bedone-byasyoudid to make sense of both the natural and the human order.)

In present terms, Mrs. Doasyouwouldbedoneby could be seen as the first, co-operative move of TIT FOR TAT, and Mrs. Bedonebyasyoudid with her birch rod is what happens next if you act badly. For instance, Tom has been naughty — he has put pebbles into the mouths of the sea anemones to fool them — so instead of getting a candy from Mrs. Bedonebyasyoudid as the other water babies do, Tom gets a pebble.

At the end of the book, the two women are revealed as one and the same person, a person who is incidentally quite a lot like George MacDonald's young-old, friendly-scary female allegories of Christian Grace in the *Curdie* books: the Victorians did love their supernatural females. This double-sided lady raises several questions. I did use to wonder why both of her avatars were married — perhaps they were too closely involved with babies to be respectable as single girls? — and where Mr. Doasyou-wouldbedoneby and Mr. Bedonebyasyoudid were to be found. Down at the pub avoiding the swarms of babies, the sickly sweet cooing, and the nasty birch-rod punish-ments, quite likely. I'm sure their two wives, or wife, had at least one offspring of her or their own, because other-wise there would have been no Mary Poppins of the P. L. Travers books — she is so obviously in the direct line of descent of the Bedoneby twins. But those questions must remain forever unanswered.

Instead I would like to ask, Why is Kingsley's Mercy-and-Justice figure female?

AS IT TURNS OUT, Kingsley's double-visaged female justice-provider has some distant ancestors. I'd like to make one of those *Star Trek*-ish hyperdrive leaps in time and space, and go back, back, back, thousands of years ago, to the Middle East. What I'm tracking is both a painted image and a constellation. The constellation is Libra, the scales or balance, and as a present-day zodiac sign it rules from September 23 to October 22. One explanation of its name is that it rises at the time of the autumnal equinox, when the day and the night are of equal length, a balance being a device for determining equivalents. A more questionable interpretation is that it appeared at harvest time, when farmers were weighing their produce for marketing purposes.

But more likely it had another origin. In Akkadian — an ancient Semitic language spoken by, among others, the Assyrians — this constellation was called *zibanitu*, which means "the claws of the Scorpion," because it rose before the constellation of the Scorpion and was thought to be the front part of it. But *zibanitu* could also mean a weighing scales — a scorpion held upside down is similar in shape to the ancient form of this device. The constellation is now known only as Libra, a Latin word meaning "scales or balance." It is usually pictured as — guess what — a scales or balance, consisting of a crossbar suspended from a central arm or chain, with a pan hanging from each end of the crossbar. It's the only zodiac sign that isn't an animal or a person, although it's frequently held by a young woman, often identified as Astraea, the daughter of Zeus and Themis. Both Themis and Astraea were goddesses of justice, and Astraea is also known as the constellation Virgo, the virgin. Thus, in the Virgo-Libra configuration, we see a young woman holding a double-armed scales and identified with Justice.

From Themis and Astraea to Mrs. Bedonebyasyoudid may seem like a stretch, but there are some other generations as well. Jumping back in space-time again, we find ourselves in Ancient Egypt, and this time we're hunting for the scales as weighing device. The scales or balance is one of the very first articulated mechanisms to appear in pictorial art based on mythology. There are many pictures of scales in the "coffin texts" found in tombs —"coffin texts" being charms and spells written on the coffin itself, or on scrolls of papyrus, intended to help the soul make its way through the Egyptian Underworld after death.

First stop on the soul's trip was the Halls of Ma'ati, where the dead person's heart would be weighed on a two-armed scale of the kind used in Ancient Egypt for weighing gold and jewels. Ma'ati meant Double Ma'at — double not in the evil-twin sense of "double," but in the times-two sense — double strength. As for Ma'at, she was a goddess, sometimes pictured as two goddesses, or a pair of twins — teenage twins, with wings on their shoulders and ostrich feathers in their headdresses. She was one of the presiding deities at the weighing of the heart, the others being jackal-headed Anubis, who did the actual weighing, and ibis-headed Thoth, moon god and thus, in a society that used the lunar calendar, the god of time. He was also the god of measurements and numbers and astronomy and engineering skills, and in addition he was a supernatural scribe or clerk. In heart-weighing scenes, he's often shown with his wax tablet at the ready and his stylus poised, just as a scribe would have been present at a real-life gold-weighing to record the results.

Sometimes a miniature Ma'at was shown sitting on one pan of the scales, but more often it was her feather — the feather of Ma'at — that was used to counterweight the heart. If your heart weighed the same as Ma'at, you could go on to the next stage and meet and merge with Osiris in his guise as god of the Underworld, where a suitable underworldly location would be assigned to you, with possibilities for rebirth. (The Egyptian inner coffin was known, reassuringly, as "that which begets," and the coffin-board was known as "the egg"— so you might hatch out of death, just like a bird.)

However, if your heart was heavier than the feather, it would be thrown to an unpleasant crocodile-headed deity, which would eat it. As with most mythologies or religions, there was a way around this moment of dreadful judgement: you could fortify your heart ahead of time with special charms obliging it not to snitch on you. Presumably the heart was willing to co-operate, since it would be better for both of you if your heart kept your dirty deeds to itself: being eaten by a crocodile was not in either of your best interests. On the other hand, your cheatin' heart might tell on you. The uncertainty must have been what made the drama of post-mortem heart-weighing such a riveting subject for speculation among the Ancient Egyptians.

Interesting that it was the heart, even so long ago, that was thought to absorb the effects of your good and bad deeds, like Dorian Gray's scoundrelly picture. It's not the heart that remembers your moral pluses and minuses, really—it's the brain. But we can't be convinced of that. No one ever sends his valentine a picture of a brain with an arrow through it; nor, in the case of romantic failure, do we say, "He broke my brain." Maybe that's because, although the brain's in the control tower, it's the heart we can feel responding to our emotions—as in, *Be still my beating heart*. (Not brain.)

Why was it Ma'at who was used as the counterweight to the heart? Ma'at was a goddess, but she wasn't a goddess with a specific function or area, such as writing or fertility or animal husbandry: she was much more important than that. The term *ma'at* meant truth, justice, balance, the governing principles of nature and the universe, the stately progression of time—days, months, seasons, years. It also meant the proper comportment of individuals toward others, the right social order, the relationship between the living and the dead, the true, just, and moral standards of behaviour, the way things are supposed to be—all of those notions rolled up into one short word. Its opposite was physical chaos, selfishness, falsehood, evil behaviour—any sort of upset in the divinely ordained pattern of things.

This concept—that there is an underlying balancing principle in the universe, according to which we should act—appears to have been almost universal. In Chinese culture, it's the Tao or Way, in Indian culture it's the wheel of karmic justice. If not in this world, then in the next, and if not now, then in the future, the TIT FOR TAT cosmic law of reciprocity would see to it that you'd be returned good for good and evil for evil.

Even in shamanistic hunter-gatherer societies, there was a right way, and failure to follow it would upset the balance of the natural world and result in famine: if you did not treat the animals you killed with respect, not killing too many of them and thanking them for giving themselves as food, and if you did not share your kill fairly, as custom demanded, the goddess of the animals would withhold those animals from you.

The protector of animals and the hunt was unambiguously female. Ancient Greek-speakers worshipped Artemis of the Silver Bow as Mistress of the Animals; there were many Celtic goddesses associated with wild animals; among the Inuit of northern Canada, Nulialiut was the feared undersea goddess who gave or withheld the seals, whales, and walruses according to the virtuous behaviour of men or the lack of it. In early Neolithic times, babies were thought to be produced by women alone, so it made sense that wild-animal fecundity would be also controlled by a female deity. This person was not a demure girly-girl: she could be ferocious, and was relentless when crossed.

However, by the time they started recording and elaborating their mythologies, the Ancient Egyptians were already agriculturalists: they depended not on wild animals but on managed herds, and on crops. Thus, although they had a number of gods with animal heads, these animals were for the most part not hunted wild prey but domesticated animals such as cows. An exception was the lion-headed goddess Sekhmet — her name means "she who is powerful"— who was in charge of a list that at first seems bewildering: war and destruction, plagues, and violent storms on the one hand, and physicians, healing, and protection from evil on the other. This double-bladed list makes sense once we know that Sekhmet was also the defender of Ma'at, so her acts of destruction were performed to avenge wrongs and to restore the rightful balance of things. She is TIT FOR TAT in action — unlike Ma'at, who doesn't perform deeds but is the standard against which they are to be measured.

Sekhmet, like Ma'at, was a daughter of the sun god Ra, the lifegiver who created the world by naming it. Sekhmet was also known as "the blazing eye of Ra," a goddess who could see injustice and then fry it. (This notion exists in the Old Testament as well — the all-seeing eye of God is usually focused on bad deeds rather than good ones.) But Sekhmet appears to have confined her activities to this life, whereas Ma'at is present everywhere. She was the *sine qua non*, that without which nothing else could exist. So, during your post-mortem trial, your heart was being weighed against nothing less than the sum total of order in the universe.

We are usually given to understand that we are the philosophical heirs of the Greek-speakers and Romans and Israelites, not of the Ancient Egyptians, but in fact the Greek tradition of divine justice is somewhat more confusing and foreign to us than the Egyptian one. The Greek-speakers had several goddesses of justice, the first being Themis, meaning "order," who represents some of the same ideas as Ma'at does. She was a Titaness — a member of that older group of ruling supernaturals who were close to the Earth itself. The Titans were overthrown by Zeus and the Olympians, but Themis weathered the transition and was given a seat on Olympus. She was an infallible prophetess, and these powers came from her ability to look into the patterns of the universe. In some accounts she has a daughter by Zeus, called Diké, or "Justice"— justice not so much of the Egyptian right-balance kind as of the punishment kind. Diké was quite aggressive, and can be seen on vase paintings hitting people with a mallet.

Another kind of justice was represented by the goddess Nemesis. She's often thought of as a goddess of retribution, but her name means, roughly, "dispenser of dues," so she was really a goddess of evening out the shares or balancing the distribution of good and bad fortune. Among her accessories were the wheel of fortune, a sword, and a scourge made of branches — like Mrs. Bedonebyasyoudid's birch rod. A third goddess of justice was Astraea, yet another daughter of Themis. Her kind of justice was more Ma'at-like — a justice of truth, right behaviour, and things running the way they should; but because men got too wicked, she could no longer stay on Earth and thus became the constellation Virgo — the girl already mentioned, she who holds those heavenly scales.

The rule with religions seems to be: take what you need from the religion preceding yours, incorporate those bits into your own religion, and dump or demonize the rest. The Roman goddess of justice was called Iustitia; she was given the weighing scales of Astraea and the sword of Nemesis — which may have once belonged to the Mesopotamian sun god Shamesh, who had both the scales for weighing out justice and the sword for enforcing it. Iustitia was also given a blindfold, so she wouldn't be influenced by the defendants' social class, and sometimes she was given a torch, symbolizing the light of truth, and sometimes she was given the Roman bundle of rods — the Fasces — that denoted civil authority. Having only two hands, she can't hold all of those things at once, so when you see her depicted outside European and North American courts of law, she will have made a choice among these objects. Usually it's the balance and the sword.

So Iustitia inherited a lot of accessories from the gods and goddesses who came before her, but she was not thought of as judging the souls of the dead. Instead, she presided over the law courts and weighed, not hearts, but the evidence before her. However, by Roman times she's an allegorical figure rather than a numinous, awe-inspiring goddess. The Ancient Egyptians really believed that there was a Ma'at, and especially that there was a Sekhmet, and that these deities could intervene with drastic results, both in this life and the next. But Iustitia is a statue representing a principle: the justice she represented was administered in human courts of law, by human beings, according to law codes that they themselves had devised.

So much for justice in this life, but what about the next one? The Greek and Roman afterlives were neither very pleasant nor very consistently described, but some sort of soul-judging and rewarding and punishing seems to have gone on down in their murky Underworlds. Being dead, however, was far from fun: as the dead hero Achilles tells the visiting, still-alive Odysseus in *The Odyssey*, better to spend one day on Earth as the meanest slave than to be king of the dead. Some folks got punished in the afterlife, it's true, but for the virtuous there was nothing like a truly delightful heaven: no gardens, harps, or virgins for them. The boring fields of asphodel were about the height of it. As for what caused men to have the fortunes and misfortunes that were meted out to them on Earth, that was the business of the Fates, against whom even the gods could not stand. The Greek-speaking ancients were heavy on the tat side of tit-for-tat — evil begot evil — but not very keen on the good-for-good part: about the best you might expect as a reward for right action was being turned into a tree.

For something closer to the Egyptian weighing of the heart, and also closer to the concept of Ma'at, we need to leap forward in time to Christianity. The ideas contained in the word *ma'at* are similar to those suggested by the Greek word *logos*, or at least by some uses of it. Logos is neither a wheel nor a balance nor a way, but a word, or *the* Word. It enters Christianity via the famous opening to the Gospel of Saint John—"In the beginning was the Word, and the Word dwelt with God, and the Word was God." But the Logos isn't any old word—it's a Ma'at-like word. It is both a god and a word at the same time: one that comprises the true, just, and moral foundations of all that exists.

Christianity has no goddesses as such. It has some female saints, many of whom are pictured holding their cut-off body parts, but though they may help you get a husband, play the piano, or find lost objects, they don't have major powers. The Virgin Mary is the strongest one, but all she can do is intercede on your behalf: she performs no devastating lionesslike acts of retribution.

However, instead of lesser gods, Christianity has angels. None are explicitly female, though they generally have long hair and no beards. At the Last Judgement, Osiris-like Christ presides over the big picture but it's the Archangel Michael who takes over the task of soul-weighing. Like Ma'at, he has wings, and he's often shown with a scales. He's inherited that Roman and sword of justice, in addition. As in the Egyptian heart-weighing scenes, there's a record keeper—the Angel Gabriel is the "recording angel," the one credited with keeping God's ledger book up to date—and it's these records that will be produced at the Last Judgement.

And maybe even before that: if Heaven is in session right now, Lazarus, poor and miserable during his earthly life, is looking over the heavenly railing at the rich man, Dives, who is frizzling and frying down below; thus the account books of happiness and suffering are being evened out. The Muslim religion also has a Last Judgement scales of justice, the *mizan* — your good deeds are weighed against your bad ones — and not one but two record books kept by angels: Raqeeb keeps the right-side one of good deeds, and Ateed the left-side one of bad deeds. With them and their documents on hand, there will be no room for that usual excuse of politicians: "I can't recall."

From the Egyptian goddesses Ma'at and Sekhmet to the Roman goddess Iustitia to the Archangel Michael to Mrs. Bedonebyasyoudid is a long journey, but if it's true that human beings don't create anything unless it's a variation of the human-behaviour modules present on their *Homo sapiens sapiens* smorgasbord, then each of these supernatural beings is a manifestation of that inner module we were talking about earlier: the one we could call "fairness," "balancing out," or "reciprocal altruism." As we sow, so shall we reap, or that's what we'd like to believe; and not only that, but someone or something is in charge of evening up the scores.

WITH THE EXCEPTION of the Christian and the Muslim ones, the supernatural justice figures I've been talking about are all female. Why is that? With the earlier goddesses, such as Ma'at and Themis, you might say they belong to or are at least descended from the Great Mother period in the Near East and the Middle East, during which the top deity was female and was also identified with Nature. But the Great Goddesses period was followed by several thousand years of rigorous misogyny, during which gods replaced goddesses and women were subordinated and downgraded. Yet the female Justice figures persisted. What accounts for their staying power?

If we were primatologists, we could point to the fact that among the chimpanzees it's often the older matriarchs who are the king-makers: the alpha male can stay in power only with their support. This tendency is even more marked among the gelada monkeys of the Ethiopian highlands, where families consist of groups of tightly bonded females, their children, and the mate they've selected, who remains the in-house family male only as long as the females say so. If we were anthropologists, we might point to the female elders in hunter-gatherer bands such as the Iroquois, who had a lot of say when an animal was being divided up and shared out among families, as they were well versed not only in relative social status but in relative need. If we were Freudians, we might talk about psychic child development: the first food comes from the mother, as do the first lessons in justice and punishment and in the fair sharing-out of goods.

Whatever the reason, Justice continues to wear a dress, at least in the Western tradition, which is a possible explanation for the attachment of our Canadian Supreme Court justices to their lovely red gowns and their wigs.

I'D LIKE TO MAKE yet one more *Star Trek* leap in time and space, and go back to a play that commemorates the moment when the meting-out of justice was transferred from powerful supernatural female beings to what was — and would long remain — a male-dominated court-of-law system. The play is *The Eumenides*, third in the trilogy known as *The Oresteia*; the author was Aeschylus; the place was Athens; and the date of presentation was 458 B.C.E., during the period of Greek history we call "classical."

The subject matter of the play comes from the earlier legendary period — the Mycenaean/Minoan era — and concerns the aftermath of the Trojan War. In the first play of this trilogy, King Agamemnon, returning from the Trojan War, is murdered by his wife, Clytemnestra, in revenge for Agamemnon's sacrifice of their daughter, Iphigenia — an act he performed in order to gain a favour-able wind for his Troy-bound ships. In the second play, *The Libation Bearers*, Orestes, the son of Agamemnon and Clytemnestra, returns from exile in disguise and, cheered on by his sister Electra, murders his mother. We are in the middle of a tit-for-tat blood feud, the rules of which are stated very clearly by Shakespeare's Lady Macbeth: "Blood will have blood." Orestes owes a blood debt of vengeance to his father, and killing his mother discharges that debt.

However, under the archaic pre-classical customs, the murder of a mother was a very sinful thing — much more sinful than Clytemnestra's murder of Agamemnon, who was not her blood relation and certainly not her mother. So Orestes has incurred another debt: his own blood is claimed in payment by the Erinyes, or "Raging Ones," known to the Romans as the Furies. They are older than the Olympian gods, being daughters of Earth and Night; they are horrible-looking, savage, and vindictive; and their task is to pursue kin-murderers and kinship-bond violators such as Orestes, and to drive them mad and force them to kill themselves.

In *The Eumenides*, Orestes has been pursued by them to the shrine of Apollo, who has purified him of blood guilt; but the Erinyes don't accept this verdict. Orestes then goes to Athens, where the goddess Athene — considering herself an insufficient judge in this complex case of father's blood weighed against mother's blood — puts together a jury of twelve Athenians to try the case, reserving the deciding vote for herself. The jury splits, and Athene casts her vote in favour of fathers and men, presenting as evidence the concept that men alone generate children, whereas women only incubate them. She cites herself as being a prime example, since she sprang fully formed from the forehead of Zeus, her only begetter. (She forgets to mention the preliminary part of her own myth, in which she got into Zeus's head in the first place because he ate her pregnant mother.)

The Raging Ones feel shamed by the Athenian verdict — three ancient matrilineal goddesses of great power have been deposed by a younger male-oriented female upstart who has never been a mother, and claims not even to have been the child of one. They threaten to curse Athens with various witchy blights, but Athene, by a mixture of flattery and bribery, cajoles them into staying on as Athens' guests. They'll still have power and worship, she says, and they'll love their new accommodations in a dark cave.

The Furies are given a new name, "the Eumenides," or "Kindly Ones." In the play, they switch from being "utterly repulsive" and disgusting smelly animal-women with tusks and bat wings and ooze-dripping blood-red eyes into gracious and stately beings, "grave goddesses"—a quick change that to the modern mind suggests those women's magazine Before and After makeover features. Thus disguised, and presumably with their tusks extracted and their bat wings concealed by a little artful drapery, the Raging Ones go off to their cosy underground shrine in a happy, singing processional. The goddesses of the primitive past have been driven down out of sight, although — as Athene points out — the possibility of blood-for-blood retribution cannot be erased altogether, because Justice must always be reinforced by Fear. Trial by jury and the rule of law have been installed, and are presented as more enlightened and more civilized, recognizing as they do the payment for injuries in currencies other than blood; and the long chain of blood feuds — by which one death leads to another, ad infinitum — will be broken.

"I will pick the finest of my citizens," says Athene, speaking of the court of justice she is about to establish

"for all time to come." "They shall swear to make no judg-
ment that is not just, and make clear where the truth of
this action lies." The tribute paid to the above-board and
the even-handed in *The Eumenides* is laudable. But
although the ancient sense of fairness is a necessary
inner foundation stone for any legal system, it doesn't
follow that every legal system is necessarily fair. Classical
Athens applied fair judgement and allowed full liberties
only to Athenian citizens, and only to male ones. Slaves
and women were excluded from citizenship, and the laws
governing them were harsh.

Despite this, and despite the millennia during which
women were excluded from courts, whether as judges
or lawyers or jurors — and in many cases, even as credi-
ble adult witnesses — the allegorical figure of Justice
remained female. She's still standing outside our court-
rooms today, holding up her scales, the survivor of a long
line of scale-wielding ancestresses.

so far i've been discussing not only the principle of fairness without which no system of borrowing and lending
could exist and the female justice figures such as Ma'at
and Themis and Astraea and Iustitia and Charles
Kingsley's punishing and rewarding Mrs. Bedoneby
twins, but also the history of balances, those two-sided
devices for determining fairness by weighing one thing
against another. In the afterlife of Ancient Egypt, the
heart was weighed against the concepts of justice and
truth, which included the right order of the cosmos and

the natural world; in the Christian system, Michael the Archangel weighs the soul against its deeds; and, going back to the bank book I had as a child, the red debits were weighed against the black credits, and the resulting figure was called "the balance." The Ancient Egyptian balance weighed moral pluses and minuses, as did the archangel's; however, the bank balance was concerned only with numbers, although it was considered a bad thing to go too far into the red: bad for you, and bad of you, as well.

In the next chapter, titled "Debt and Sin," I'll be asking the question, Is being a debtor morally bad? Is it in fact sinful? And if so, how sinful, and why? And, since a debtor is one-half of a twinship — the other twin being the creditor — I'll also ask, Is being a creditor sinful, as well?

TWO

DEBT AND SIN

"DEBT IS THE NEW FAT," someone said recently. Which led me to reflect that, not so long ago, fat was the new cigarette-smoking, and before that, cigarette-smoking was the new alcohol-drinking, and before that, alcohol-drinking was the new whoremongering. And whoremongering is the new debt; and so we go in circles. What all these things have in common is that at one time or another each has been considered the very worst sin of all but has then gone through a period of being thought, if not totally harmless, at least fashionable. I left out hallucinogenic drugs, though they fit in there too.

We seem to be entering a period in which debt has passed through its most recent harmless and fashionable period, and is reverting to being sinful. There are even debt TV shows, which have a familiar religious-revival ring to them. There are accounts of shopaholic binges during which you don't know what came over you and everything was a blur, with tearful confessions by those who've spent themselves into quivering insomniac jellies of hopeless indebtedness, and have resorted to lying, cheating, stealing, and kiting cheques between bank accounts as a result. There are testimonials by families and loved ones whose lives have been destroyed by the debtor's harmful behaviour. There are compassionate but severe admonitions by the television host, who here plays the part of priest or revivalist. There's a moment of seeing the light, followed by repentance and a promise never to do it again. There's a penance imposed — *snip, snip* go the scissors on the credit cards — followed by a strict curb-on-spending regimen; and finally, if all goes well, the debts are paid down, the sins are forgiven, absolution is granted, and a new day dawns, in which a sadder but more solvent man you rise the morrow morn.

Once upon a time, people took the utmost precautions to avoid going into debt in the first place. There were various once-upon-a-times — as I've said, debt goes in and out of fashion, and today's admired free-spending gentleman is tomorrow's despised deadbeat. But the time I have in mind was the Great Depression, which my parents lived through as a young married couple. My mother had four envelopes, into which she put the money from my father's paycheque every month. These envelopes were labelled *Rent, Groceries, Other Necessities,* and *Recreation.* Recreation meant the movies. The first three envelopes had priority, and if there was nothing left for the fourth envelope, there were no movies, and my parents went for a walk instead.

My mother kept an account book for fifty years. I notice that in the early years of their marriage — the late 1930s, the early 1940s — they sometimes went into debt — fifteen dollars here, fifteen dollars there — or took out small loans from the bank — fifteen dollars here, fifteen dollars there. Not such small sums either, come to think of it, when the bread bill for the entire month was a dollar twenty and the milk bill was six dollars. The debts are always paid back within weeks, or a few months at the latest. Once in a while an odd item appears —"Book," two dollars and eighty cents; "Luxury foods," forty cents. I wonder what the luxury foods were? I suspect they were chocolates — my mother told me that if they happened to come by any chocolates, they would cut each one in two so they could both sample all the flavours. This was called "living within your means," and judging from the debt TV shows, it's a lost art.

AS THE TITLE of this chapter is "Debt and Sin," I'd now like to recall the moment when I first connected the two. This happened in a church — specifically the United Church Sunday School, to which I insisted on going despite the trepidations of my parents, who were worried that I might get religiously addled too early in life. But I was religiously addled already, since in my part of Canada at the time there were two taxpayer-funded school systems, the Catholic and the public. I was in the public one, which was interpreted then to mean Protestant, so we did a certain amount of praying and Bible-reading right in the classroom, presided over by a portrait of the King and Queen of England and Canada in crowns and medals and jewellery, watching us benevolently from the back of the room.

Since we had religion in the classroom, my Sunday-school caper was an add-on. As usual, I was propelled by curiosity: wouldn't I find out more about religious knowledge in a Sunday school than I could in an ordinary school? Not likely, as it turned out — the most interesting parts of the Bible, those dealing with sex, rape, child sacrifice, mutilations, massacres, the gathering up in baskets of the lopped-off heads of your enemy's kids, and the cutting up of concubines' bodies and sending them around as invitations-to-a-war were studiously avoided, though I did spend a lot of time colouring in angels and sheep and robes, and singing hymns about letting my little candle shine in my own small, dark corner.

It will no doubt astonish you to learn that I won a prize for memorizing Bible verses, but such was the case. Among the things we memorized was the Lord's Prayer, which contained the line, "Forgive us our debts as we forgive our debtors." However, my brother sang in an Anglican boys' choir, and the Anglicans had a different way of saying the same line: "Forgive us our trespasses as we forgive those that trespass against us." The word "debt"— blunt and to the point — was well fitted to the plain, grape-juice-drinking United Church, and "trespasses" was an Anglican word, rustling and frilly, that would go well with wine-sipping for Communion and a more ornate theology. But did these two words mean the same thing really? I didn't see how they could. "Trespassing" was stepping on other people's property, especially if there was a *No Trespassing* sign, and "debt" was when you owed money. But somebody must have thought they were interchangeable. One thing was clear even to my religiously addled child mind, however: neither debts nor trespasses were desirable things to have.

Between the 1940s and now, the search engine has providentially come into being, and I've recently been trolling around on the Web, looking for an explanation of the discrepancy between the two translations of these Lord's Prayer lines. If you do this yourself you'll find that "debts" was used by John Wycliffe in his 1381 translation and "trespasses" in Tyndale's 1526 version. "Trespasses" reappears in the 1549 English Book of Common Prayer, though the King James 1611 translation of the Bible reverts to "debts." The Latin Vulgate uses the word for "debts." But it's interesting to note that in Aramaic, the Semitic language that was spoken by Jesus, the word for "debt" and the word for "sin" are the same. So you could translate this word as "Forgive us our debts/sins," or even "our sinful debts," though no translator has chosen to do this yet.

If you keep searching on the Web, you'll come upon quite a few sermonlike blog postings. What their authors generally end up saying is that the debts and/or trespasses mentioned in the Lord's Prayer are *spiritual* debts and/or trespasses. They are, in fact, sins: God will forgive the sins we've committed in proportion as we ourselves forgive those sins committed against us.

We are warned by the sermonizing bloggers against making the naive mistake of believing that the debts in question are actual money debts. Here is an excerpt from a blog posting from the Reverend Jennie C. Olbrych of the lovely old Saint James Santee Episcopal Church near McClellanville, South Carolina — I know it's lovely and old because there's a picture of it on the web site — and this posting hits all the nails on the head, one after the other.

"Here I am reminded of the Lord's prayer," says Reverend Olbrych, "...and remember that financial debt is sometimes a metaphor for sin — forgive us our sin, trespasses, debts as we forgive those who sin, trespass, or are indebted to us..."

Owing a lot of money is fairly typical these days — 2.5 trillion $ in consumer debt as of June this year.... The average household owes close to $12,000 in credit card debt. If you are a homeowner, you will know that signing a home mortgage or big note is sobering... overwhelming if you think about it too much....

In another church I served, I had a couple come for some pastoral counselling...they were fighting like mad...and somewhere along the way I asked them how much debt they were carrying — it was close to $75,000 in credit card debt...their annual income was somewhere around $50,000. They were overcome by debt and could not hope to pay it off....Think how relieved they would have been if someone from MasterCard, the person who had been harassing them

previously, called out of the blue and said...we're going
to write off that debt. Or, if someone called and said...the
bank is going to forgive your home mortgage...or
your student loan debts...or your business debt...we're
going to forgive it...you'd probably be thinking...this
is too good to be true, no way this is legal...it's probably
a mistake at the bank...and you'd probably wait and
then check your balance...and then the statement arrives
in the mail...or better, yet, the deed...free and clear...
what a celebration that would be! Wouldn't you be prais-
ing American Express or Visa, or the bank to the high
heavens...because debt really is a form of slavery—

Now, some of you who are practical folks no doubt
would be saying—well, that's nice idea but that can't
work practically because the whole system would fall
apart...if everybody's mortgages were forgiven, the
banking system would collapse...someone has to
pay...and you are right to think this...

To become debt free is a wonderful thing—but
more wonderful is to become debt free in a spiritual
sense...

Here, in one nicely compact bouquet of meanings, we
have: financial debt as a metaphor for sin; the horror and
the burden of being in debt; the joy we would experience
if all our debts of the financial kind were suddenly to be
written off; the impossibility of that actually happening
in the world of practical affairs, because "the whole system would fall apart"; and the notion that debt is a form

of slavery. If we connect the end to the beginning, we get an even neater equation: financial debt is not only a metaphor for sin, it is a sin. It's a debt/sin, as in the original Aramaic.

Modern-day preachers stop well short of saying that the truly virtuous thing would be for creditors to simply burn their record books, but there's good reason for believing Jesus meant that we should forgive financial debts as well as sins of other kinds. Not only did he use a word that to him meant both, but he was well aware of Mosaic law, by which a sabbatical year had to be proclaimed every seven years in which all debts should be cancelled. "At the end of every seven years thou shalt make a release," says Deuteronomy 15:1 and 2. "Every creditor that lendeth ought unto his neighbour shall release it; he shall not exact it of his neighbour, or of his brother, because it is the Lord's release."

Why, you might ask, would anyone ever lend anything to anyone else under these circumstances? Probably because the lendings and borrowings took place within small communities. You didn't have to wipe out the debts owed to you by foreigners — only those within the group, where relations with the next-door neighbours were cradle-to-grave and tightly knit, and he who was the lender one year might find himself the borrower the next. My mother, who grew up in a small community in Nova Scotia, used to say, "In a village everyone knows your business." A good reputation was very important in such places, and nobody wanted to be known as a person who did not repay, or they might not get a cup of flour or an egg the next time they needed one. So you'd ultimately be repaid somehow for a forgiven debt, even if it wasn't with money. During the Great Depression, for instance, few in rural Nova Scotia had cash to spare, but my grandfather — the local doctor — got paid anyway, in chickens and wood. They certainly did get sick of chicken, said my mother, but at least they were never cold.

IN HER 1994 BOOK, *Systems of Survival*, Jane Jacobs proposes the theory that there are only two ways in which human beings acquire objects: taking and trading. Everything we do in the way of accumulation falls under one of these two heads, says Jacobs, and we should never confuse the two. We should be especially careful to prevent experts in one area from being put in charge of the other. For instance, police officers — who belong to the guardianship of the "taking" end and have the weaponry we allow to such guardians — should not also be the merchants, or bribery and protection rackets and other forms of corruption will be the result.

Using Jacobs's two headings, under "taking" would come hunting and fishing and gathering, and looting during a war, and acquisition of territory by force, and robbery, and rape, and forcing people into slavery, and finding pennies on the sidewalk or — as I prefer to do — paper clips. Under "trading" would come barter, and buying and selling, and arranged marriages, and treaties governing market rules, though these latter are sometimes "taking"— gunboat diplomacy, it used to be called. When I first read this book, I became obsessed with identifying transactions that would not fit into this double-headed scheme. At first I thought of gifts: surely a gift is neither taken nor traded. But no: gifts fit under "trading," because although no set price is attached to a gift and it is bad form as well as bad luck to sell one, a rule of exchange is still at work: for a gift you owe, at the very least, a payment of gratitude; and in addition to that, you owe a gift of your own, if not to the person who gave you the first gift, at least to someone else. Artistic gifts work like this. An artistic talent is bestowed or given — it cannot be bought — and further inspiration comes from other artists through their work to you and is then passed on to someone else through your own work, should you be so lucky.

But what about borrowing and lending? Borrowing and lending would seem to exist in a shadowland — neither "taking" nor "trading"— changing their natures depending on the final outcome. They're like those riddles in fairy tales: *Come to me neither naked nor clothed, neither on the road nor off it, neither walking nor riding.* A borrowed object or sum is neither taken nor is it traded. It exists in a shadowland between the two: if the interest exacted for a loan is of loan-shark magnitude, the transaction verges on theft from the debtor; if the object or sum is never returned, it also verges on theft, this time from the creditor. Thus it's "taking," not "trading." But if the object is borrowed and then returned with a reasonable amount of interest, it's clearly trading. Hostage-taking is the same kind of shadowland transaction: part theft or taking, part trade.

THERE IS, HOWEVER, another kind of ambiguous financial arrangement: pledging an item that may be redeemed, or bought back, at a later time. Or it may not be bought back, in which case whoever is holding the object is allowed to keep it. Pledging is a very old practice. For instance, Deuteronomy 24: 6 says, "No man shall take the nether or the upper millstone to pledge: for he taketh a man's life to pledge." Much of Deuteronomy is taken up with laws governing fairness — laws that set a limit on how far you're allowed to go. Not taking a millstone meant that you couldn't take away something a man needed in order to earn his living, because — obviously — he would never then be able to pay his debt to you and get the millstone back. Thus taking away a man's main tools as a pledge was as bad as stealing. And if it was a small household mill, you'd literally be taking the bread from the family's mouths.

This kind of intermediate transaction is still very much with us. We call the pledging of items "pawning," and we do it in establishments called "pawnshops." These places have a whiff of brimstone about them, as anything existing in the shadowland between clear categories risks having.

MY AUNT JOYCE Barkhouse of Nova Scotia, who is now ninety-five, tells the following story involving a pawnshop.

When my brother was born, in mid-February 1937 —
in the depths of the Great Depression — there was a
special Valentine's Day excursion price on the train from
Nova Scotia to Montreal. It cost ten dollars. My aunt and
a girlfriend scraped together the ten dollars each and
went to Montreal to help out my mother with her new-
born baby. When they got there, my mother was still in
the hospital, because my father hadn't received his
monthly paycheque and thus couldn't pay the bill and
bail her out, hospitals at that time having a lot in common with debtors' prisons. My father was finally able to
spring my mother, but paying the hospital bill — ninety-
nine dollars, as I found from looking in my mother's
account book — used up all of the paycheque.

My parents didn't have a bean at that time, so my
father had no cash reserves, and he pawned his fountain
pen in order to take my aunt out for a thank-you lunch.
(The fact that he felt the need to do this shows that he
understood the need for a gift of gratitude in return for
a gift of care and service, which was what my aunt had
bestowed.) When my aunt and her friend took the train
back to Nova Scotia, they were also given two valuable
going-away presents: a bunch of grapes and a small box
of Laura Secord chocolates — and this is all they had to
eat during the train ride. They had no berths, so they had
to sit up the whole time, and this was uncomfortable; but
a man was renting pillows for twenty-five cents each.
Alas, they had only forty-eight cents between the two of
them, but they offered the forty-eight cents and two of

the chocolates — fluttering their eyelashes, said my aunt — and their offer was accepted. Thus they slept in comfort.

When I heard this story as a child, I rejoiced at the successful securing of the pillows, and remembered the lesson of the haggling procedure: if you don't offer a deal, you won't get one. Later, having become interested in pens, I thought, What kind of fountain pen was it? And considering the fact that my parents didn't have a bean, how could my father have had a fountain pen that was expensive enough to pawn? Still later, I marvelled at the cheapness of the train trip — ten dollars would hardly get you a bottle of water and a few potato chips now — and the high value placed on the bunch of grapes.

But now I think, My father! That man of rectitude! Going into a pawnshop! How incongruous! Indeed, this part of the story was told in a hushed but delighted tone, as if the pawnshop episode was disreputable — like sneaking into a girly show — and transgressive — some line had been crossed — but also courageous and self-sacrificing: look what my father was willing to put himself through in order to do the right thing!

When I was very young, I used to think that pawnshops had something to do with chess — you could buy extra pawns there to replace those that were always vanishing down behind the sofa cushions. But this is not the case. The chess kind of pawn comes from "peon," or peasant — the pawns are the foot soldiers, and you send them out first and make pawn sacrifices with them because they're worth relatively little. The pawnshop kind of pawn comes from a word meaning "pledge"— you leave something in the pawnshop and the pawnshop owner gives you some money and a ticket with a number on it, and you can come back later and "redeem," or buy back, your item by presenting the ticket and paying the original sum, plus extra for the use of the money and the cost of the transaction. But if you don't come back with the cash within a stated period, you lose your right to buy the thing back, and the item belongs to the pawnbroker, who can sell it and keep the profit.

As for why pawnshops had a seedy reputation by the time my father went into one with his fountain pen, opinions are mixed. As with anything that has two sides and involves the balance between them — a scale for weighing the soul against the feather of truth, a dispute over mother-murder versus father-murder, a good-deeds recording angel and a bad-deeds one, your monthly budget or the good and bad effects of pawnshops — it's hard to get the two sides exactly equal.

PAWNSHOPS GO BACK at least to classical Greece and Rome, and, in the East, to 1000 B.C.E. in China. The negative view of them comes from their reputation as the last resort of down-and-outers and the suspicion that robbers used them to dispose of stolen goods: pinch something, sell it to the pawnbroker, then just never come back to collect it. There was another dodge too: a man intending to go bankrupt or skip town could buy goods on credit, pawn them, and then take off with the cash.

The positive version is that pawnshops are happy-to-help do-gooders for the unwealthy, a sort of poor man's banker: both the Franciscans of the Middle Ages and the Buddhist monks of Ancient China ran pawning operations for the benefit of the poor. Such pawnbrokers would provide tiny sums that those without a lot of collateral couldn't borrow from the more pompous lending bodies: in effect, they were microfinancers. Saint Nicholas is the patron saint of pawnbrokers — there's a touching legend whereby he provides dowries for three poor girls who can't get married without them, and the dowries were three bags of gold — hence the three gold balls you see hanging outside every Western pawnshop. (In China it's not three gold balls, it's a good-luck bat — but that's another story.)

There's nothing whatsoever to the other legend about Saint Nicholas — that he comes down the chimney every December 25 with a sackful of stuff he's nicked from the pawnshop. It is however true that the nineteenth-century colloquial expression "Old Nick" — meaning the Devil — is directly connected with Saint Nicholas. There are other clues. Note the red suit in the case of each; note the hairiness, and the association with burning and soot. We get the slang term "to nick," meaning "to steal," from…But I digress, pausing simply to add that Saint Nicholas, as well as being the patron saint of young children, those sticky-fingered elfin creatures with scant sense of other people's property rights, is also the patron saint of thieves. Saint Nicholas is always found in the vicinity of a big heap of loot, and when asked where he got it he'll tell an implausible yarn involving some non-human labourers hammering away in a place he euphemistically calls his "workshop." A likely story, say I.

As for those three gold-coloured balls, the dowry story is lovely, but a more substantial account is that the balls were part of the armorial bearings of the Medicis, who were very rich; and that they were then adopted by the House of Lombard, bankers and lenders who wanted people to think they were very rich; and quite soon — because this early form of suggestive advertising and sympathetic magic worked — they *were* very rich.

AMONG THE FIRST things that people were able to pawn were other people. The Code of Hammurabi of Meso-potamia, which dates from about 1752 B.C.E., is a set of amendments to existing laws, which means that debt law itself is even older. By reading this code, we learn that a man in debt could pawn his wife and his kids, and his concubines and their children, and his slaves, as debt slaves to a merchant in return for money to repay his debt; or else he could sell his household members out-right. In the latter case, he couldn't redeem them: they'd remain slaves for life. But if they were put up as pledges for a loan and the loan was repaid within a certain period, the debt slaves would be restored to him. He could also — if he was really desperate — sell himself into debt slavery, in which case he'd most likely stay a slave because no one would come forward to redeem him.

Debt slavery is by no means a thing of the distant past. Consider present-day India, where a man may be a virtual debt slave all his life — many get into this position through having to provide dowries. Think, too, of the smuggling of illegal immigrants from Asia into North America, where the person smuggled is told he has to work without wages forever in order to pay off the cost of his travel experience. In the nineteenth century, in the mining villages of northern Europe, the company store supplied the place of the slave owner: the miners had to buy their food and the necessities of life from the store, where these things cost more than the miners could ever earn.

In Émile Zola's most celebrated novel, *Germinal* — named for one of the new month-names brought in by the French Revolution, Germinal being April — this system is described in all its sordid and gritty detail. The store manager is a nasty man with the age-old view that sex is a marketable commodity, so he takes the debt out in trade, using the wives and daughters of the miners for this lecherous purpose. You'll be pleased to learn that there's a famous riot scene in which the wives and daughters get their revenge, and the genital organs of the store owner are skewered on a stick that's carried in triumphant procession through the streets — a crude form of entertainment, granted, but there was no TV then. Another form of nineteenth-century debt slavery was that practised by those who rented rooms and clothing to prostitutes, or ran brothels in which the girls' food and clothing were charged on a running tab that could never be worked off. Some form of this is still going on, although the cost of addictive drugs has been added onto the running tab. All of these means of keeping people bound to your will and working for bare subsistence wages are recipes for despair: they're a nightmare treadmill that you can never get off.

By the time the Code of Hammurabi was written down, slavery itself had been going on for a long time. Where did it come from? In *The Creation of Patriarchy*—by "patriarchy" is not meant genial Dad sitting at the head of the table carving up the Sunday roast, but the system by which it was a man's right to treat his wife or wives and children as if he owned them absolutely and could dispose of them at will, like chairs and tables—Gerda Lerner has this to say: "Historical sources on the origin of slavery are sparse, speculative, and difficult to evaluate. Slavery seldom, if ever, occurs in hunting/gathering societies but appears in widely separated regions and periods with the advent of pastoralism, and later agriculture, urbanization, and state formation. Most authorities have concluded that slavery derives from war and conquest. The sources of slavery commonly cited are: capture in warfare; punishment for a crime; sale by family members; self sale for debt; and debt bondage.... Slavery could only occur where certain preconditions existed: there had to be food surpluses; there had to be means of subduing recalcitrant prisoners; there had to be a distinction (visual or conceptual) between them and their enslavers." She goes on to postulate that the first slaves were women, because they could be more easily controlled, and that male war captives were usually just brained or shoved off a cliff until someone thought of the clever device of blinding them — thus giving us Samson Agonistes, in John Milton's poem of the same name: "...eyeless in Gaza, at the mill with slaves."

Samson is an Old Testament hero whose God-given strength depends on his not divulging his secret, which is that he'll lose all his power if his hair is cut off. And it is cut off, by a treacherous woman — they leak like a sieve, those women; don't tell them anything unless you want the neighbours to hear. But Samson redeems himself from his enemies and tormenters — he buys back the freedom of his soul — at the cost of his own physical life. How fascinating that we say a person "redeems himself" when he's been guilty of a disgraceful action and then balances it out with a good or noble one. There's a pawnshop of the soul, it appears, where souls can be held captive but then, possibly, redeemed; and that is what I'd like to discuss next.

FIRST, A CURIOUS manifestation of this pawnshop of the soul: the Sin Eater. The custom of sin-eating appears in a 1924 novel by Mary Webb called *Precious Bane*, the title of which comes from John Milton's *Paradise Lost*, Book I. After his fall from Heaven into Hell, Satan sends out a mining expedition:

There stood a Hill not far whose griesly top
Belch'd fire and rowling smoak; the rest entire
Shon with a glossie scurff, undoubted sign
That in his womb was hid metallic Ore,
The work of Sulphur. Thither wing'd with speed
A numerous Brigad hasten'd. As when bands
Of Pioners with Spade and Pickaxe arm'd
Forerun the Royal Camp, to trench a Field,
Or cast a Rampart. MAMMON led them on,
MAMMON, the least erected Spirit that fell
From heav'n, for ev'n in heav'n his looks & thoughts
Were always downward bent, admiring more
The riches of Heav'ns pavement, trod'n Gold,
Then aught divine or holy else enjoy'd
In vision beatific: by him first
Men also, and by his suggestion taught,
Ransack'd the Center, and with impious hands
Rifl'd the bowels of thir mother Earth
For Treasures better hid. Soon had his crew
Op'nd into the Hill a spacious wound
And dig'd out ribs of Gold. Let none admire
That riches grow in Hell; that soyle may best
Deserve the pretious bane.

Thus we know by its title that Webb's *Precious Bane*
will have as one of its themes a destructive obsession
with riches; and so it does. It's set in nineteenth-century
Shropshire, where old folkways have lingered on. Gideon
Sarn's father has died of a stroke, with his boots on — an

unlucky thing, as he was assumed to have died "in his wrath, with all his sins upon him," the way Hamlet wants his murderous stepfather Claudius to die. You could pay off your debt of sins by a true repentance, but if you haven't had time to do that, you're cooked. That's when you need a Sin Eater. The narrator explains:

> Now it was still the custom at that time, in our part of the country, to give a fee to some poor man after a death, and then he would take bread and wine handed to him across the coffin, and eat and drink, saying,
>
> I give easement and rest now to thee, dear man, that ye walk not over the fields and down the by-ways. And for thy peace I pawn my own soul.
>
> And with a calm and grievous look he would go to his own place. Mostly, my Grandad used to say, Sin Eaters were such as had been Wise Men or layers of spirits, and had fallen on evil days. Or they were poor folk that had come, through some dark deed, out of the kindly life of men, and with whom none would trade, whose only food might oftentimes be the bread and wine that had crossed the coffin. In our time there were none left around Sarn. They had nearly died out, and they had to be sent for to the mountains. It was a long way to send, and they asked a big price, instead of doing it for nothing as in the old days.

It's the dead man's son Gideon who acts as the Sin Eater in *Precious Bane*; he does so to get hold of the family farm, which he intends to work within an inch of its life so he can get rich and lord it over everyone. But his sin-eating brings bad luck to him: his drinking of the Sin Eater's wine is described thus: "He took up the little pewter measure full of darkness..." Uh-oh, we think. No good will come of this. If a Sin Eater's motives are pure and selfless, he has some hope of escaping the curse. But not if his "looks and thoughts / Are only downward bent." As Gideon's are.

Sin-eating was also known in the Scottish Border Country, and in Wales. Lewis Hyde, in his book *The Gift: Imagination and the Erotic Life of Property*, describes a similar but not identical Welsh custom of a century ago:

> The coffin was placed on a bier outside the house near the door. One of the deceased's relatives would then distribute bread and cheese to the poor, taking care to hand the gifts over the coffin. Sometimes the bread or cheese had a piece of money inside it. In expectation of the gift, the poor would have earlier gathered flowers and herbs to grace the coffin.

Hyde classes funeral gifts with a larger class he calls "threshold gifts"—gifts that help the passage from one state of life to another. In the Welsh custom, the dead person is being helped to get from this life to the next, and if this is not done properly he may be trapped on Earth as a ghost—ghosts being, notoriously, souls with unfinished business here on Earth. There are similar customs all over the world, and objects placed in burial sites or pyramids had the same function: they accompanied the journey and helped the transition. Next time you throw a flower into an open grave, ask yourself why you're doing it.

But something extra is added with sin-eating. The bread and wine handed across the coffin is an obvious echo of the Christian communion. That sacramental meal is thought to place the soul in a state of grace, but the sin-eating bread and wine had the opposite effect: what you ate and drank was darkness, not light. The Sin Eater was thought to assimilate all the sins he'd eaten, thus freeing the souls of the dead from them, and as such he has obvious connections with scapegoat figures. He'd also pawned his own soul, as a guarantee that someone — namely himself — was prepared to pay for all those sins when the time for payment came.

However, although he'd pawned his soul, the Sin Eater hadn't sold it. He'd placed it in hock, in return for the bread and wine and money, to be sure, but also in an act of courageous risk, because — as in a game of Pass the Parcel — should he himself die with his boots on, and should no Sin Eater appear for him, he'd get stuck with the entire bundle of sins. The pawnbroker was the Devil, of course: it was he who'd collect the pawned soul, unless the soul of the Sin Eater was redeemed just as you'd redeem a pawned object from the shop. It's worth remarking here that a "pawn" could also have the meaning of "a hostage." Hostages then — as they are today — were people held in captivity, to be exchanged either for other people or for sums of money. The Sin Eater's soul thus acted as a hostage as well as a substitute for the soul of the man whose sins he'd eaten. No wonder the Sin Eater in *Precious Bane* goes to "his own place" with "a calm and grievous look."

The first hostage of this sort that we know about in mythology would appear to be Geshtinanna, from the Sumerian myth of Inanna. The life-goddess Inanna loses a power struggle with Erishkigal, the goddess of Death, and is killed. But it won't do for the goddess of Life to be dead — bad for the garden, not to mention every other living thing on Earth — so another god makes two golemlike robotic beings who are not organically alive, and therefore not subject to death. These rescue Inanna and bring her back to the light. However, Erishkegal says that the number of the dead must remain complete or the cosmic balance will be upset, so a substitute has to be found to take Inanna's place in the Sumerian underworld. The victim is the shepherd-king Dumuzi, Inanna's mortal consort. But Dumuzi's sister Geshtinanna offers herself as a substitute, and the gods are so impressed with her spirit of self-sacrifice that they split the death term — six months underground for Dumuzi, and six for Geshtinanna. Geshtinanna is thus probably the first example of one individual redeeming another through offering herself as a substitute, which is the essential idea of the Sin Eater: something is owed; the person who owes it can't pay; then someone else steps forward and pays the debt, or takes the place of the indebted one. The parallels with Christianity are obvious.

Every human pattern exists in both a positive and a negative version. In the negative version of this pattern, instead of offering up yourself as a substitute for someone else, you offer up someone else as a substitute for you. A good example of the negative version may be found in George Orwell's dystopian novel *1984*. The hapless protagonist, Winston Smith, has been sent to the dreaded Room 101. Room 101 always contains the worst thing in the world, which in Winston's case happens to be rats. The rats have been starved, and are about to be let loose on his eyes.

> The mask was closing on his face. The wire brushed his cheek. And then — no, it was not relief, only hope, a tiny fragment of hope. Too late, perhaps too late. But he had suddenly understood that in the whole world there was just one person to whom he could transfer his punishment — one body that he could thrust between himself and the rats. And he was shouting, over and over:
>
> "Do it to Julia! Do it to Julia! Not me! Julia! I don't care what you do to her. Tear off her face, strip her to the bones. Not me! Julia! Not me!"

Julia, by the way, is Winston's beloved mistress. This substitution of another for yourself is a very familiar concept to students of early religions, as it lies behind the practice of both animal sacrifice and human sacrifice. You owe a debt to the gods, so let something or someone else pay it for you. Readers of the Old Testament will find—especially in Leviticus and Deuteronomy—long lists of what animal you can have ritually killed in payment for which sin, trespass, or guilt of your own, or in repayment for an especially large favour granted by God. This animal redeems that one: you can for instance redeem a first-born donkey with a lamb, which must be killed in its place.

The sacrifices in the Middle East and Greece could be human ones, at least for important occasions. King Agamemnon, leader of the Trojan War expeditionary forces, sacrifices his daughter, as the Old Testament military leader Jephthah sacrifices his: what both of them get in return is victory. Joshua, after his conquests of Canaanite cities, slaughtered all the captives and also their animals as an offering to God, just as Elijah slaughters the 450 priests of Baal. The first-born of any species, including the human species, was thought to belong to God in any case—thus Abraham's lack of surprise when God tells him to sacrifice his only son, Isaac. The introduction of animal substitution for human victims is said to be illustrated by this story, as in the event it's a ram rather than a child that gets its throat slit. However, human sacrifice—mostly of children—was a widespread practice in the ancient world; and these were substitution sacrifices, redeeming the debts you owed or paying the gods for favours. Instead of yourself, you offered up a suitable bit of your property—a bull, a dove, a child, a slave—muttering all the while some version of "Do it to Julia."

Happily, by the time of the Book of Numbers, money equivalents could be offered instead. Think of that the next time you drop your envelope into the collection plate at church. That twenty-dollar bill is a substitute for your getting your throat cut, and cheap at the price.

WHICH BRINGS US to the Christian religion. Christ is called the Redeemer, a term drawn directly from the language of debt and pawning or pledging, and thus also from that of substitute sacrifice. In fact, the whole theology of Christianity rests on the notion of spiritual debts and what must be done to repay them, and how you might get out of paying by having someone else pay instead. And it rests, too, on a long pre-Christian history of scapegoat figures — including human sacrifices — who take your sins away for you.

Here's the condensed version, and I apologize if through having squashed it into so short a form I don't do it full justice:

God gave Man life and was therefore owed a debt of absolute gratitude and obedience. Man, however, did not repay this debt as he should have done, but reneged on it through an act of disobedience. In this way he put himself and his descendants permanently in hock — for, as we know if we've ever dealt with wills, a person's debts devolve on the heirs and assigns of the debtor. As regards the built-in debt of sin, the creditor is sometimes thought to be Death, sometimes the Devil: this entity collects either (a) your life or (b) your soul — or both — as payment for the debt you yourself still owe due to your rascally distant ancestor.

The debt load of sin you've inherited from Adam — "Original Sin," as it's known — which has been added to through your own probably not very original sins — can never be repaid by you, because the sum total is too large. So unless someone steps forward on your behalf, your soul will become (a) extinct or (b) a slave of the Devil in Hell, to be disposed of in some unpleasant way. Various of these ways are described by Dante, where Hell is ruled over by a really horrible version of Gilbert and Sullivan's Mikado, ingeniously bent on making the punishment fit the crime. If that's too medieval for you, a shorter rendition can be had in the sermon on Hell incorporated into James Joyce's *A Portrait of the Artist as a Young Man*.

During their lifetimes, all souls not in a state of grace or actually sold to the Devil fully and finally are believed to be in an intermediate condition: in peril, but not fully damned as yet. Christ is thought to have redeemed all souls, in theory at least, by having acted as a cosmic Sin Eater — he took everyone else's sins upon himself at the Crucifixion, where, with Geshtinanna-like selflessness, he offered himself up as the substitute human sacrifice to end all substitute human sacrifices — thereby redeeming the huge Original Sin debt. But individuals must also participate in this drama: in effect, you must redeem yourself by allowing yourself to be redeemed.

Thus all the souls of the living can be thought of as residing in a pawnshop of the soul, neither entirely slaves nor entirely free. Time is running out. Will you be redeemed before the clock strikes midnight and the Grim Reaper arrives — or, worse, Old Nick in his red suit, ready to pop you into his infernal collecting sack? Hang by your fingertips! It's never over till it's over!

This is what gives the Christian life its dramatic tension: you never know. You never know, that is, unless you're a believer in the Antinomian Heresy. If you are, you're so certain of your own salvation that even the most despicable things you do are right, because it's you doing them. Here's a summation of this position, taken from a 2005 article in the London *Telegraph* in which the author, Sam Leith, suggests that Tony Blair, the ex–prime minister of England, was in the grip of this heresy:

Roughly put, antinomianism — and this will have to be roughly put, since I make no claim to be a theologian — is the idea that justification by faith liberates you from the need to do good works. Righteousness overrides the law — which was, arguably, the PM's position on Iraq.

It can be seen, in some way, as the squaring of a tricky theological circle: the Calvinist idea that the Elect have been singled out for salvation as part of the divine scheme long before any of them were twinkles in the twinkles in their ancestors' eyes. If justification by faith, rather than by works, is the high road to heaven, the logical extreme of the position is that works don't matter at all.

Divine grace, over which we have no control, brings about faith. Faith brings about salvation. Ergo, if you're not touched by grace, there's nothing much you can do about it except look forward to an immensely long retirement having your toes warmed by the devil in the pitchfork hotel.

If, on the other hand, you are one of the Elect, whoop de doo: Jesus wants you for a sunbeam and no amount of bad behaviour is going to prevent him seeing you right. This is a pretty crazy view to take, most of us would agree, and historically it has tended to be discouraged by both civic and religious authorities for rather obvious reasons. But there it is.

Since politicians, at least in the English-speaking West, are showing an increasing tendency to drag religion into politics, it would seem fair for the electorate to be able to question them on their own theological views. "Do you believe that you personally are irrevocably saved, that any graft, fraud, lying, torturing, or other criminal activities you may engage in are fully justified because you're one of the Elect and can do no wrong, that to the pure such as yourself all things are pure, and that the vast majority of those you say you wish to represent as their political leader are vile and worthless and predestined to fry in hell, so why should you give a damn about them?" would seem to be an appropriate lead-off at question time.

THERE'S A NOVEL that explores the Antinomian Heresy very thoroughly: James Hogg's 1824 *The Private Memoirs and Confessions of a Justified Sinner.* It's no coincidence that in this day of holier-than-thou politicians it's attracting increased critical attention. Here's the situation: religiously warped by a fanatical mother, sure that he's predestined to be redeemed, and filled with envy and hatred, specifically for his more attractive brother and his jolly old tippler of a dad, the narrator commits one foul crime after another, led on by a mysterious stranger whom he encounters just when he becomes fully convinced of his own irrevocable membership in the Elect.

A prop considered necessary in any respectable literary early-modern pact with the Devil is the Infernal Book, for reasons we'll come to later; and in Hogg's novel it duly makes its appearance. One of his first encounters with the mysterious stranger is in a church, where the enigmatic one is found reading something that at first glance looks like a Bible:

> I came up to him and addressed him, but he was so intent on his book that, though I spoke, he lifted not his eyes. I looked on the book also, and still it seemed a Bible, having columns, chapters, and verses; but it was in a language of which I was wholly ignorant, and all intersected with red lines and verses. A sensation resembling a stroke of electricity came over me, on first casting my eyes on that mysterious book, and I stood motionless. He looked up, smiled, closed his book, and put it in his bosom. "You seem strangely affected, dear

sir, by looking at my book," said he mildly. "In the name of God, what book is that?" said I. "Is it a Bible?"

"It is my Bible, sir," said he.

Quite soon the mysterious stranger starts talking of blood bonds, and we readers know who he is: for the blood bond and the shockingly bad book are two unmistakable attributes of the fifteenth-to-nineteenth-century Devil — the literary one, at least — who tempts you into making a contract with him that you have to sign with your own sanguinary fluid. Hogg's evil book seems to be a satanic version of Scripture, though more usually the Devil's tome is an account book, in which the souls of the already-purchased are noted down, ready to be collected when the fatal moment comes. Céline has a novel called *Death on the Installment Plan,* and that is in effect what the Devil is selling: you buy now, you enjoy the benefits of whatever goodies the Devil provides, and then you pay later, forever.

Patrick Tierney, in his fascinating book *The Highest Altar: The Story of Human Sacrifice,* comments on the different — and older — traditions that prevail among the shamans — or *yataris* — of the Lake Titicaca region in South America.

Here the very masochistic, and Christian, notion of selling your own soul to the devil in exchange for a treasure never caught on — or made much sense. The Aymara yatari's more practical approach was to sell someone else

to the devil, "body and soul"...the way to avoid harm
in making a pact with the devil was simply to give the
devil a human victim....Obviously, someone is physi-
cally killed in this diabolical exchange. Not so obvious,
however, is the sinister underlying deal whereby the
soul of that person is permanently enslaved....

In former times, before the coming of Europeans to
this region, the sacrificial victim — usually a young,
innocent person or child — was mentally and emotionally
prepared in advance, feasted and flattered and convinced
to take on the role willingly, thus becoming a volunteer
guardian spirit for all — a powerful conduit for spiritual
forces that served the entire community. In this way the
victim was akin to the Sin Eater, and thus to the scapegoat: a taboo figure, "accurst," as the Sin Eater in *Precious
Bane* is called, but also blessed; a figure who after his sacrificial death was revered, approached with fear and
trembling, and given sacrifices in his or her turn.

Among present-day Lake Titicaca *yataris* and their
customers, however — says Tierney — individual pacts
with the local deities are undertaken for selfish ends
involving worldly wealth and power, and the victim is far
from willing. In fact, he or she is lured to the sacrificial
spot and murdered, and the soul is enslaved and made
to do whatever the entrapper wants. Those performing
the sacrifices are said to live in fear of the souls escaping
and then wreaking vengeance, like Spartacus or the
wives and daughters in *Germinal* — resentment at unfair

treatment being a universal unpaid debt that cries out for a balancing of the scales.

Early in human history, lists of such offerings to the supernatural forces, and pacts with them, and debts owing to them, wouldn't have been set down in permanent form. But with writing came records, and books, and contracts. The envisioning of the unseen world tends to mirror what's available on Earth: the gatherings of witches pictured by seventeenth-century New Englanders, for instance, bore an eerie resemblance to the Puritan church meetings of the same period. So the Devil got hold of his writing implements as soon as human beings got hold of theirs; in fact, he may even have inherited them from earlier post-mortem scorekeepers, such as the Egyptian scribe god Thoth.

The Devil's chosen medium has changed over the years. Sometimes it's not an actual book that requires signing with your blood; sometimes it's a scroll, or a deed of gift, as in Christopher Marlowe's late-sixteenth-century play *The Tragical History of Doctor Faustus*. But whatever its physical form, it's a contract, and signing it causes your name to be written down in the bad book, just as the names of the righteous are written down in the good one. Since the Devil is among other things a lawyer—the lawyer for the prosecution, you might say—he's very fond of contracts, and also of records and account books.

WHY THE NEED for so much documentation? Let's consider the link between debts and written records.

Without memory, there are no debts: a debt is some-thing owing for a transaction that's taken place in the past, and if neither debtor nor creditor can remember it, the debt is effectively extinguished. "Forgive and forget," we say; and, in fact, we may not be able to forgive totally *unless* we forget. Hell, in Dante's *Divine Comedy*, is the place where absolutely everything is remembered by those in torment, whereas in Heaven you forget your personal self and who still owes you five bucks and instead turn to the contemplation of selfless Being. Or that's the theory.

Without memory there's no debt, granted; but we can remember stories — and thus grudges and debts of hon-our, and who needs to be revenged on whom — anything about people and their doings — much more easily than we can remember long strings of numbers, unless we are mathematical geniuses. Our advanced mathematical abil-ity is very recent, and far from instinctual: the times tables are hammered into our heads through memorizing alone, and even when you've learned them you sometimes resort to counting on your fingers — in the days before calculators, that is. The Barbie doll that got into trouble for saying "Math is hard" was just telling the truth. So most of us require a technical assist to perform our calcu-lations, even if it's only a piece of paper and a pencil.

But how did we conduct our business affairs before we had that piece of paper? How, for instance, did we trade? We've been trading physical items for at least forty thou-sand years, the archaeologists tell us, but without some sort of recordkeeping, trading over long distances must have been risky. To be sure you were getting the value you wanted, trades had to be done face to face — your obsidian for my ochre. Middlemen were undependable: what was sent might not always be what was received, and there would be no sure method of proving it either way. But once devices for recording the transactions were in place, a go-between merchant could do your trading for you and bring back the proceeds, and you could check up on the numbers.

All human technologies are extensions of the human body and the human mind. Thus eyeglasses and telescopes and the images of television and film and painting are extensions of the eye, the radio and telephone of the voice, the cane and crutch of the leg, and so on. Writing and written numbers are — among other things — extensions of the memory. These *aides-mémoire* appeared independently in many human societies, and methods for transmitting numbers, and thus debts, seem always to have appeared before written-down poetic and religious materials: such emotion-and-narrative-driven works could more easily exist in oral form.

Among the Inca of South America, bunches of knotted coloured strings — called *khipu* — were used for this purpose. In early Mesopotamia, small clay cones, balls, cylinders, and other geometrical forms were sealed into clay envelopes. These shapes have now been identified as symbols representing herd animals — cows, calves, sheep, lambs, goats, kids, donkeys, and horses. The envelope could be sent with the herdsman, and could not be opened without being broken. Thus, whoever had already bought the animals had a certified account or waybill.

Cuneiform tablets came later; the vast majority of them are accounting records and inventories, since by this time the priest-kings of Mesopotamia were in the grain-surplus business and had set up the first banks, which were food banks. With the food surpluses came large-scale warfare: you can't feed armies without them. And with the wars came more inventories, much needed when it came to dividing up the loot. The first thing Genghis Khan's armies did after a city surrendered was to take inventory, not only of all the valuables, but of all the people. Genghis Khan typically massacred the rich and the aristocracies, but he saved the scribes: he needed a huge bureaucracy in order to run his empire, and literacy came in handy.

Recordkeeping, and thus the ability to track debits and credits, allowed sophisticated taxation systems to proliferate. Initially, taxation was a sort of protection racket: if the taxes were paid to the religious establishment, you were supposed to get the protection of the gods; if they were paid to a king or emperor, you were supposed to get the protection of his armies. Taxes fell most heavily on the peasants — those who produced the actual food that kept the superstructure going — and so it remains today. In theory, taxes are different from someone merely walking into your house and taking your stuff. That's called "robbery," whereas with taxes you're supposed to be getting something in return. What exactly you do get in return provides the chattering points for many a modern election.

When they first appeared, written records must have seemed like black magic to the illiterate: strange markings they couldn't read could be produced against them by lawyers and landlords, and thus such objects acquired an evil reputation. This is where the Devil's infernal account book most likely comes from. Indeed, the Devil of the early modern period bears more than a passing resemblance to a tax collector or punitive landlord, waving around infernal soul-for-money contracts like the stage villain of melodrama come to extract the overdue rent and molest the teenage daughter. Although the Bible says, "The wicked borroweth and payeth not again," it must have seemed to the wretched of the Earth that it was the creditor rather than the debtor who was truly wicked.

All of which goes to answer the question, What is it that Ebenezer Scrooge's underpaid clerk, Bob Cratchit, is scratching away at all day in his dismal little tank of an office? It's the accounts — the accounts of the debts owed to Scrooge, the mortgager and merciless moneylender. As the Archangel Gabriel is to God, Bob Cratchit is to Scrooge: for where there are debts, there must be memory, and the memories of Scrooge that are initially important to him are of the debts owed to him, and it's Bob's quill pen that's turning these into records.

Traditionally, it was in poor areas where the financial laws weighed heavily that destroying such records was a longed-for dream, and where cheating the landlord and the taxman and the moneylender was considered not only a right but a virtue. Robin Hood the outlaw and thief is a hero, the money-gathering Sheriff of Nottingham and King John the rapacious creditor and tax extortionist are villains. Robert Burns wrote a short poem called "The Deil's Awa' wi' the Exciseman," in which the Devil dances away with the man sent to collect taxes on the villagers' home-brewed malt whisky. Old Nick is given a hearty thanks for this act of snatch-and-grab, since it's a case of the worst creditor in the world making off with a miniature version of himself, and good riddance to both of them.

WHICH IS MORE blameworthy — to be a debtor or to be a creditor? "Neither a borrower nor a lender be," says the tendentious Polonius of Shakespeare's *Hamlet* to his impatient son, Laertes, "for loan oft loses both itself and friend / And borrowing dulls the edge of husbandry." In other words, if you lend a friend some money and he doesn't pay you back, you'll end up being angry with him, and he with you. And if you borrow, you'll be spending money that isn't yours and that you haven't earned, rather than managing within your income. Good advice, Polonius! Strange that so few people follow it. Or possibly strange that anyone at all still follows it, since we are constantly told that borrowing is actually laudable because it turns the wheels of "the system," and that spending lots of consumer money keeps some large, abstract, blimpish thing called "the economy" afloat.

But Polonius had it right: when the borrower/lender scales are too severely out of balance for too long, resentment builds, each side becomes despicable in the eyes of the other, and debt is revealed as a double-sided balancing act in which debtor and creditor alike are culpable. "To wipe the slate clean" is a colloquial expression meaning to atone for your sins and make reparation for whatever you've done wrong, but the metaphor — like all metaphors — is based on something in real life: the slate in bars and pubs where regular customers' running tabs were recorded. A dirty slate is dirty because it's smeared all over with debts, of one kind or another; but it's dirty for both debtor and creditor alike.

I'll end with two ambiguous epigraphs from the vast grab bag of English folk sayings — one for debtors and one for creditors. For debtors: "Death pays all debts." For creditors: "You can't take it with you." Neither one of these is strictly true — debts can linger after death, and "You can't take it with you" depends on what "it" is — but that's another story. And it's to that other story — or rather to debt as a primary engine of story itself — that I will turn in my next chapter, which is called "Debt as Plot."

(THREE)

DEBT AS PLOT

WITHOUT MEMORY, there is no debt. Put another way: without story, there is no debt.

A story is a string of actions occurring over time — one damn thing after another, as we glibly say in creative writing classes — and debt happens as a result of actions occurring over time. Therefore, any debt involves a plot line: how you got into debt, what you did, said, and thought while you were in there, and then — depending on whether the ending is to be happy or sad — how you got out of debt, or else how you got further and further into it until you became overwhelmed by it, and sank from view.

The hidden metaphors are revealing: we get "into" debt, as if into a prison, swamp, or well, or possibly a bed; we get "out" of it, as if coming into the open air or climbing out of a hole. If we are "overwhelmed" by debt, the image is possibly that of a foundering ship, with the sea and the waves pouring inexorably in on top of us as we flail and choke. All of this sounds dramatic, with much physical activity: jumping in, leaping or clambering out, thrashing around, drowning. Metaphorically, the debt plot line is a far cry from the glum actuality, in which the debtor sits at a desk fiddling around with numbers on a screen, or shuffles past-due bills in the hope that they will go away, or paces the room wondering how he can possibly extricate himself from the fiscal molasses.

In our minds — as reflected in our language — debt is a mental or spiritual non-place, like the Hell described by Christopher Marlowe's Mephistopheles when Faust asks him why he's not in Hell but right there in the same room as Faust. "Why, this is Hell, nor am I out of it," says Mephistopheles. He carries Hell around with him like a private climate: he's in it and it's in him. Substitute "debt" and you can see that, in the way we talk about it, debt is the same kind of placeless place. "Why, this is Debt, nor am I out of it," the beleaguered debtor might similarly declaim.

Which makes the whole idea of debt — especially massive and hopeless debt — sound brave and noble and interesting rather than merely squalid, and gives it a larger-than-life tragic air. Could it be that some people get into debt because, like speeding on a motorbike, it adds an adrenalin hit to their otherwise humdrum lives? When the bailiffs are knocking at the door and the lights go off because you didn't pay the hydro and the bank's threatening to foreclose, at least you can't complain of ennui.

Scientists tell us that rats, if deprived of toys and fellow rats, will give themselves painful electric shocks rather than endure prolonged boredom. Even this electric shock self-torture can provide some pleasure, it seems: the anticipation of torment is exciting in itself, and then there's the thrill that accompanies risky behaviour. But more importantly, rats will do almost anything to create events for themselves in an otherwise eventless time-space. So will people: we not only like our plots, we need our plots, and to some extent we are our plots. A story-of-my-life without a story is not a life.

Debt can constitute one such story-of-my-life. Eric Berne's 1964 bestselling book on transactional analysis, *Games People Play*, lists five "life games"— patterns of behaviour that can occupy an individual's entire lifespan, often destructively, but with hidden psychological benefits or payoffs that keep the games going. Needless to say, each game requires more than one player — some players being consciously complicit, others being unwitting dupes. "Alcoholic," "Now I've Got You, You Son of a Bitch," "Kick Me," and "See What You Made Me Do" are Berne's titles for four of these life games. The fifth one is called "Debtor."

Berne says, "'Debtor' is more than a game. In America it tends to become a script, a plan for a whole lifetime, just as it does in some of the jungles of Africa and New Guinea. There the relatives of a young man buy him a bride at an enormous price, putting him in their debt for years to come." In North America, says Berne, "the big expense is not a bride but a house, and the enormous debt is a mortgage; the role of the relatives is taken by the bank. Paying off the mortgage gives the individual a purpose in life." Indeed, I can remember a time from my own childhood — was it the 1940s? — when it was considered cute to have a framed petit-point embroidered motto hanging in the bathroom that said *God Bless Our Mortgaged Home*. During this period, people would have mortgage-burning parties at which they would, in fact, burn the mortgage papers in the barbecue or fireplace once they'd paid the mortgage off.

I pause here to add that "mortgage" means "dead pledge"—"mort" from the French for "dead," "gage" for "pledge," like the part in medieval romances where the knight throws down his glove, thus challenging another knight to a duel — the glove or gage being the pledge that the guy will actually show up on time to get his head bashed in, and the accepting of the gage being a reciprocal pledge. Which should make you think twice about engagement rings, since they too are a gage or pledge — what actually are you pledging when you present such a ring to your one true love? (Or, these days, your one in a series of true loves. As a friend of mine said at a wedding, "He'll make a very good *first* husband.")

But back to mortgages. With a mortgage, the house is the thing being pawned — it's put up as the gage — but the pledge becomes "dead" once the mortgage has been discharged. I like the word "discharge" here too — it's what is said of an arrested person when he or she is let out of jail.

So "paying off the mortgage" is what happens when people play the life game of "Debtor" nicely. But what if they don't play nicely? Not-nice play involves cheating, as every child knows. But it's not always true that cheaters never prosper, and every child knows that too: sometimes they do prosper, in the playground and elsewhere.

Thus there is a not-nice, cheating form of "Debtor." "'Try and Collect" is what Berne calls it, and the name says it all. Like the other cheating games in his book, the not-nice player wins something no matter what happens. Basically, the debtor obtains a lot of things on credit and then avoids paying. As with Berne's other disingenuous games, "Try and Collect" needs at least two players, and the person playing opposite the debtor is of course the creditor. If the creditor becomes too frustrated and gives up, thus failing to collect what is owed, the debtor gets something for nothing. If the creditor persists in his efforts to collect, the game becomes an exciting chase. If the creditor becomes really serious and resorts to extreme measures — court cases and the like — the debtor feels justified anger because the creditor is being so mean and grasping. The debtor can then position himself as a put-upon victim and paint the creditor as a truly bad person, who, because of his badness, does not deserve to be paid.

The obtaining of goods on credit, the avoidance of payment, the thrill of the chase, the anger at the creditor, and the acting out of victimhood all come with their own jolt-of-brain-chemical rewards, and each also performs the function of providing a key element in a story-of-my-life game of "Debtor" plot line. As the dilapidated tramp Vladimir in Beckett's play *Waiting for Godot* says of an unpleasant scene he's just witnessed, it passes the time. His pal Estragon replies that the time would have passed anyway. Yes, says Vladimir, but it would not have passed so rapidly. Whatever else debt may be, it can also — it seems — have entertainment value, even for the debtor himself. Like the rats and their self-induced electric shocks, we'd rather have something painful happening to us than nothing happening to us at all.

DEBT CAN HAVE another kind of entertainment value when it becomes a motif, not in a real-life plot line, but in a fictional one. How this kind of debt plot unfolds changes over time, as social conditions, class relations, financial climates, and literary fashions change; but debts themselve have been present in stories for a very long time.

I'd like to begin by interrogating a familiar character — a character so familiar that he's made it out of the fiction in which he stars into another kind of stardom: that of television and billboard advertising. That character is Ebenezer Scrooge, from Charles Dickens's *A Christmas Carol*. Even if you haven't read the book or seen the play or the several movies made about Scrooge, you'd probably recognize him if you met him on the street. "Give like Santa, save like Scrooge," say the ads, and we then have a lovable, twinkly old codger telling us about some great penny-pinching bargain or other.

But, wanting to have it both ways, the ads conflate two Scrooges: the reformed Scrooge, who signals the advent of grace and the salvation of his soul by going on a giant spend-o-rama, and the Scrooge we see at the beginning of the book — a miser so extreme that he doesn't even spend any of his money-hoard on himself — not on nice food, or heat, or warm outfits — not anything. Scrooge's abstemious gruel-eating lifestyle might have been applauded as a sign of godliness back in the days of the early bread-and-water saintly ascetic hermits, who lived in caves and said *Bah! Humbug!* to all comers. But this is not the case with mean old Ebenezer Scrooge, whose first name chimes with "squeezer" as well as with "geezer," whose last name is a combination of "screw" and "gouge," and whose author disapproves mightily of his ways:

> Oh! But he was a tight-fisted hand at the grindstone, Scrooge! a squeezing, wrenching, grasping, scraping, clutching, covetous old sinner! Hard and sharp as flint, from which no steel had ever struck out generous fire; secret, and self-contained, and solitary as an oyster. The cold within him froze his old features, nipped his pointed nose, shrivelled his cheek, stiffened his gait; made his eyes red, his thin lips blue; and spoke out shrewdly in his grating voice.... No warmth could warm, no wintry weather chill him. No wind that blew was bitterer than he, no falling snow was more intent upon its purpose, no pelting rain less open to entreaty....

> Even the blindmen's dogs appeared to know him; and
> when they saw him coming on, would tug their own-
> ers into doorways and up courts; and then would wag
> their tails as though they said, "No eye at all is better
> than an evil eye, dark master!"

That Scrooge has — consciously or not — made a pact with the Devil is signalled to us more than once. Not only is he credited with the evil eye, that traditional mark of sold-to-the-Devil witches, but he's also accused of worshipping a golden idol; and when, during his night of visions, he skips forward to his own future, the only comment he can overhear being made about himself in his former place of business is ". . . old Scratch has got his own at last, hey?" Old Scratch is of course the Devil, and if Scrooge himself isn't fully aware of the pact he's made, his author most certainly is.

But it's an odd pact. The Devil may get Scrooge, but Scrooge himself gets nothing except money, and he does nothing with it except sit on it.

Scrooge has some interesting literary ancestors. Pact-makers with the Devil didn't start out as misers — quite the reverse. Christopher Marlowe's late-sixteenth-century Doctor Faustus sells his body and soul to Mephistopheles with a loan document signed in blood, collection due in twenty-four years, but he doesn't do it cheaply. He has a magnificent wish list, which contains just about every-thing you can read about today in luxury magazines for gentlemen. Faust wants to travel; he wants to be very,

very rich; he wants knowledge; he wants power; he wants to get back at his enemies; and he wants sex with a facsimile of Helen of Troy. Helen of Troy isn't called that in the luxury men's magazines — she has other names — but it's the same sort of thing: a woman so beautiful she doesn't exist, or, worse, may be a demon in disguise. Very hot though, as they say.

Marlowe's Doctor Faustus isn't mean and grasping and covetous. He doesn't want money just to have it — he wants to dispense it on his other wishes. He's got friends who enjoy his company, he's a big spender who shares his wealth around, he likes food and drink and fun parties and playing practical jokes, and he uses his power to rescue at least one human being from death. In fact, he behaves like Scrooge, after Scrooge has been redeemed — the Scrooge who buys huge turkeys, giggles a lot, plays practical jokes on his poor clerk, Bob Cratchit, goes to his nephew's Christmas party and joins in the parlour games, and saves Bob's crippled offspring, Tiny Tim, leading us to wonder if Scrooge didn't inherit a latent gene for bonvivantery from his distant ancestor Doctor Faustus — a gene that was just waiting to be epigenetically switched on. (Scrooge doesn't get sex with a pretend Helen of Troy, however. He's too wrinkly for that. Having thrown over his fiancée because she didn't have enough money and then having devoted himself to no sins but those of the counting house, he's left that part of life too long. All he gets is a moment of ogling the cute young maid at his nephew's house —"Nice girl! Very!" says he, Hugh

Hefnerishly — but even this ogling is done in an avuncular and benevolent manner: no bottom-pinching or even cheek-pinching for Scrooge.)

Was Dickens consciously writing Scrooge as a reverse Faustus? He'd have known the Faust tale through the English pantomime — he was a devoted pantomime fan, and Faust was still popular on that stage in the days before *A Christmas Carol* was written. There are so many correspondences it's hard to avoid the thought: Faustus longs to fly through the air and visit distant times and places, Scrooge dreads it, both do it. Both have clerks — Wagner and Bob Cratchit — the one treated well by Faustus, the other treated badly by Scrooge. Both attend jolly parties in invisible form, at which Faustus behaves disruptively and Scrooge behaves well. Marley is Scrooge's Mephistopheles figure who carries his own Hell around with him, but he's come to save Scrooge's soul, not to buy it; the three ghosts of Christmas past, present, and future play his attendant spirits, though they're angelic rather than demonic; and so forth. Everything Faustus does, Scrooge does backwards. I'm sure somebody has investigated this subject more thoroughly, and if so, I'd be happy to be informed of the results.

The next important Faust after Marlowe's was of course Goethe's, and his Faust is also expansive in his desires; it's this version that gives rise to the Gounod opera featuring the seduction of the unfortunate Marguerite via some very sparkly jewellery. Goethe's Faust is ultimately redeemed, unlike Marlowe's; but in this, Goethe was not inventing something new, as there are earlier stories in which the pacter-with-the-Devil achieves redemption. It's not the big-spending, high-living, knowledge-seeking branch of the pact-with-the-Devil family from whom Scrooge is immediately descended, however. For Scrooge's miserly daddy or granddaddy, we must turn to an American author, Washington Irving.

Dickens is known to have proclaimed his fondness for Washington Irving, a writer of the generation before his who was very well known by Dickens's time. Irving is best remembered for his creepy tale "The Legend of Sleepy Hollow," the one with the Headless Horseman in it; but he wrote lots of other stories, and Dickens was familiar with them. One of them is called "The Devil and Tom Walker." In this version of the Faustean pact, the pact-maker shows none of the love of luxury and largesse that branded earlier Fausts as worldly and therefore damned. Instead he's the most miserly creature imaginable. He and his equally stingy wife live in a swamp in which some pirate treasure is hidden, and one day Tom comes across a black man — not, Irving emphasizes, a man who is black, but more like a blackened man, for his blackness comes from soot. This creature is rapidly identified by Tom:

> "Since the red men have been exterminated by you white savages," says the blackened man, "I amuse myself by presiding at the persecutions of quakers and anabaptists; I am the great patron and prompter of slave dealers, and the grand master of the Salem witches."

"The upshot of all which is, that, if I mistake not," said Tom, sturdily, "you are he commonly called Old Scratch."

And so he is. Tom and Old Scratch come to terms: Old Scratch will show Tom where the pirate gold is hidden in exchange for the usual body-and-soul payment, but he insists that Tom must invest the money in a business of the Devil's choosing. He wants Tom to go into the slave trade, but that's too horrible even for Tom, so they settle on moneylending.

Tom Walker set up as a usurer in Boston. His door was soon thronged by customers. The needy and the adventurous; the gambling speculator; the dreaming land jobber; the thriftless tradesman; the merchant with cracked credit; in short, every one driven to raise money by desperate means and desperate sacrifices, hurried to Tom Walker.

Thus Tom was the universal friend of the needy, and he acted like a "friend in need"; that is to say, he always exacted good pay and good security. In proportion to the distress of the applicant was the hardness of his terms. He accumulated bonds and mortgages; gradually squeezed his customers closer and closer; and sent them at length, dry as a sponge from his door.

In this way he made money hand over hand; became a rich and mighty man, and exalted his cocked hat upon change. He built himself, as usual, a vast house, out of ostentation; but left the greater part of it unfinished and unfurnished out of parsimony. He even set up a carriage in the fullness of his vain glory, though he nearly starved the horses which drew it; and as the ungreased wheels groaned and screeched on the axle trees, you would have thought you heard the souls of the poor debtors he was squeezing.

This is the Scrooge pattern: enormous amounts of money, sharp deal-making, the ruthless grinding of those in need, empty ostentation coupled with miserliness: Scrooge, like Tom, lives in a vast house that is sparsely furnished. But unlike the pre-ghost Scrooge, Tom knows that his soul is in danger, and takes to churchgoing and Bible-toting to protect himself from the Devil's collection agency. He slips up, however — he summons the Devil with a careless oath, is caught without his Bible, and is carried away by the blackened man and never seen again.

As soon as this happens, all his wealth vanishes: his bonds and mortgages are found "reduced to cinders," his gold and silver has turned to chips and shavings, the horses that once pulled his rickety carriage are skeletons, and his huge house burns to the ground. Washington Irving learned a great deal from folklore: in tales about visits to the land of the Fairies, the gold they're given is traditionally found to be lumps of coal once the sun rises — leading us to wonder how many of these tales arose from experiences people had while under the influence of hallucinogenic substances. The wrong kind of wealth, we are shown, is a similar kind of intoxicated illusion, and vanishes with either of (a) death or (b) waking up in the morning with a terrible hangover.

Scrooge's wealth is like this. The third spirit to visit Scrooge — the Ghost of Christmas Yet to Come — shows him a vision of what his own death will be like if he stays on his present course. For instance, there's a den of thieves where, in a masterful parody of Scrooge's own counting house, Scrooge's former servants are selling his worldly goods to a fence, who's duly chalking up the sums owed, in best accounting practice. The goods are "a seal or two, a pencil-case, a pair of sleeve-buttons, and a brooch of no great value"; also the shirt Scrooge was to have been buried in — removed from the corpse itself — and his blankets, and the bed-curtains. That's the lot. Somebody must have inherited Scrooge's enormous wealth, but we are not told about this in the story. Instead we're told about the cat tearing at the door and the rats gnawing beneath the hearthstone, and Scrooge's corpse upon the bed, "plundered, and bereft, unwatched, unwept, uncared for..." It's a vision of absolute poverty, both material and spiritual.

But as we know, Scrooge is saved at the end of the story, whereas Doctor Faustus, a much more generous and considerate creature, has his body torn into pieces and his soul carried off to Hell. Why is it that the signs of Scrooge's salvation — the turkey-buying and so forth — take the same form as the signs of Faustus's damnation? Maybe it's because, when Marlowe was writing, the set of

ideal Christian virtues that had held sway during so many
earlier centuries — the disdain for wealth, the asceticism,
the willed poverty, the turning of the back upon the
world — was still close enough in time to be recognizable
as a pattern of saintliness. In those days, the official religious version was that it was easier for a camel to pass
through the eye of a needle than for a rich man to enter
into Heaven, and the rich man burning in Hell while the
poor man gloated down from Heaven was still an image
dwelt upon in sermons, if only to make the rich disgorge
in favour of the Church.

But between Marlowe and Dickens fell the full triumph of the Protestant reformation in England — a
movement that had begun earlier, that had taken an
English form with Henry the Eighth's break with the
Pope and his subsequent disbanding of the monasteries,
and that by Marlowe's era was incarnate in Elizabeth the
First as head of the Church in England. The Protestants
continued to gain ground over the next two centuries,
and by the nineteenth century, although the land-based
English aristocracy still had much power, the merchants
and industrialists were replacing them as the biggest
plutocrats. How was wealth to be viewed? Was it a sign
of God's blessing, as it had been in the days of Job, or was
it, on the other hand, a precious bane — a sign of worldli-
ness and corruption, as in the days of the ascetics and
hermits? This was a debate that had been going on within
and among various branches of the Christian faith for a
long time. The camel squeezing through the eye of the

needle was impossible on Earth, some argued, but in Heaven all things are possible, so why couldn't you have both a fat bank account and a seat at the divine post-mortem banquet? "By their fruits ye shall know them," says Jesus, who clearly meant spiritual fruits; but these fruits were suspected by some apologists to be also material, and being rich was viewed by them as a sign of God's blessing and favour — a position not without its adherents in certain fundamentalist circles of America today.

The other thing that happened during the Protestant reformation was that usury — which originally meant the charging of any interest on loans — was no longer formally forbidden to Christians. Christian bankers had previously got round the prohibition by calling what they made from their trade by other names — as Muslim bankers do today — but now the lid came off the box. After Henry the Eighth, interest-charging was legalized for Christians in England, and then later for Christians in other countries; and many leapt with alacrity into that marketplace. Attempts were made to limit the amounts that could be charged, but these attempts were not entirely effective, and they still aren't — thus giving us loan sharks and daily interest rates on credit card borrowings.

In the nineteenth century, capitalism exploded in the West, scattering fiscal shrapnel hither and yon. Few people understood exactly how capitalism functioned. It seemed a great mystery — how some people got very rich without doing anything that used to be called "work" — and the superstitious might well believe that some hand other than a human one had stuck its infernal finger in the pie and helped the prosperous but surely wicked capitalist to pull out the plums. Without any regulating mechanisms, there were frequent boom-and-bust cycles; and as there were no social safety nets, there was widespread suffering during the busts. Fortunes were made by those who were in a position to profit from the roundabouts and swings — it was in the centuries after the prohibition on interest-charging was abolished that usury changed its meaning from mere interest-charging to exorbitant interest-charging — and Tom Walker and Ebenezer Scrooge, moneylenders both, are among the profiteers.

The recent fundamentalist Christian Church — especially in the American South — has identified sinning largely with sins of the flesh — especially sexual sins — though excessive drinking and drug-taking feature in there as well. The Catholic Church has also been in the sin-as-sex business for quite a long time. Whatever the intent, the effect has been to divert attention from money sins to sexual ones. But neither Washington Irving nor Charles Dickens are having any of that. Both Tom Walker and Ebenezer Scrooge are sexually abstemious: their sins are entirely due to the worship of Mammon, he of the golden calf.

The ghost of Scrooge's former business partner, Marley, displaying the principles of post-mortem heart-weighing worthy of the Ancient Egyptians and also of medieval Christianity, has to pay after death for Marley's sins during life. None of these sins involved a dalliance with Helen of Troy; all of them came from the relentless business practices typical both of Scrooge and of unbridled nineteenth-century capitalism. Marley totes a long chain made of "cash-boxes, keys, padlocks, ledgers, deeds, and heavy purses wrought in steel." He is fettered, he tells Scrooge, by the chain he forged in life — yet another example of the imagery of bondage and slavery so often associated with debt, except that now the chain is worn by the creditor. Indulging in grinding, usurious financial practices is a spiritual sin as well as a material one, for it requires a cold indifference to the needs and sufferings of others, and imprisons the sinner within himself.

Scrooge is set free from his own heavy chain of cashboxes at the end of the book, when, instead of sitting on his pile of money, he begins to spend it. True, he spends it on others, thus displaying that most treasured of Dickensian body parts, an open heart; but the main point is that he does spend it. The saintly thing in earlier times would have been for him to have given the whole packet away, donned sackcloth, and taken up the begging bowl. But Dickens has nothing against Scrooge's being rich: in fact, there are quite a few delightful rich men in his work, beginning with Mr. Pickwick. It's not whether you have it; it's not even how you get it, exactly: the post-ghost Scrooge, for instance, doesn't give up his business, though whether it remained in part a moneylending business we aren't told. No, it's what you do with your riches that really counts.

Scrooge's big sin was to freeze his money; for money, as all students of it recognize, is of use only when it's moving, since it derives its value entirely from whatever it can translate itself into. Thus the Scrooges of this world who refuse to change their money into anything else are gumming up the works: currency is called "currency" because it must flow. Scrooge's happy ending is therefore entirely in keeping with the cherished core beliefs of capitalism. His life pattern is worthy of Andrew Carnegie — make a bundle by squeezing and grinding, then go in for philanthropy. We love him in part because, true to the laws of wish-fulfilment, which always involve a free lunch or a get-out-of-jail card, he embodies both sides of the equation — the greedy getting and the gleeful spending — and comes out of it just fine.

Was Dickens conscious of the meaning of Scrooge's first name? Ebenezer means "rock that helps," which points to both the good and the bad sides of Scrooge: the hard, unyielding, cold Bad Scrooge and the good, helping Scrooge that emerges. Bad Scrooge does what in our more selfish moments we ourselves might prefer to do — hog everything for ourselves and sneer at beggars. Good Scrooge does what we sincerely hope we'd do if only we had enough cash: we'd share the wealth and save all the Tiny Tims of this world.

But we don't have enough cash. Or so we keep telling ourselves. And that's why you lied to the charity worker at your door and said, "I gave at the office." You want it both ways. Just like Scrooge.

SCROOGE IS pre-eminently a nineteenth-century figure, and it's the nineteenth century in which debt as plot really rages through the fictional pages.

When I was young and simple, I thought the nineteenth-century novel was driven by love; but now, in my more complicated riper years, I see that it's also driven by money, which indeed holds a more central place in it than love does, no matter how much the virtues of love may be waved idealistically aloft. Heathcliff of *Wuthering Heights* loves Cathy passionately and hates his rival, Linton, but the weapon with which he is able to act out his love and his hate is money, and the screw he twists is debt: he becomes the owner of the estate called Wuthering Heights by putting its owner in debt to him. And so it goes, through novel after novel. The best nineteenth-century revenge is not seeing your enemy's red blood all over the floor but seeing the red ink all over his balance sheet.

THE PSYCHOLOGISTS OF the twentieth century got some of their inspiration not only from ancient myths but also from the artists of the nineteenth century. It was Freud's opinion that "the poets"— by whom he meant not poets alone but narrative creators of all kinds —"in their knowledge of the mind, are far in advance of us everyday people." Freud himself owed a lot to the Greek-language playwrights and to Biblical sagas, but also to Ibsen; Jung was steeped in Germanic folk tales, but also in anima-dramas such as the ballets *Giselle* and *Swan Lake*. For less ethe-real or subterranean concerns — for Adlerian power dynamics, and for how who owes what to whom plays out in society — you could do worse than to consult a select batch of nineteenth-century quasi-realistic novels.

For instance, the most perfect illustration of Eric Berne's devious version of "Debtor" — the version called "Try and Collect" — is to be found in Thackeray's best-known work, the 1848 novel *Vanity Fair*. In it, we watch the grim business of poor Amelia Sedley's family bank-ruptcy, but we also watch the brilliant but socially inferior adventuress and gold-digger, Becky Sharp, claw her way up the status ladder by marrying dashing younger-brother aristocrat but ne'er-do-well Rawdon Crawley. Crawley, having annoyed his family by marry-ing Becky, and having thus been cut off from family funds, makes his living as a card sharp and billiards expert. In the chapter called "How to Live Well on Nothing a Year," Thackeray goes into considerable detail about the Crawley household's financial arrangements. Essentially, Becky and Rawdon charm the tradesmen with their top-drawer manners and their social standing and, as a result, the tradesmen sell them things on credit — things for which they never get paid. Becky in particular is a con-summate player of "Try and Collect." Thackeray comments:

> I wonder how many families are driven to roguery and
> to ruin by great practitioners in Crawley's way? — how

many great noblemen rob their petty tradesmen, condescend to swindle their poor retainers out of wretched little sums and cheat for a few shillings? When we read that a noble nobleman has left for the Continent, or that another noble nobleman has an execution in his house — and that one or other owes six or seven millions, the defeat seems glorious even, and we respect the victim in the vastness of his ruin. But who pities a poor barber who can't get his money for powdering the footmen's heads; or a poor carpenter who has ruined himself by fixing up ornaments and pavilions for my lady's *déjeuner*; or the poor devil of a tailor whom the steward patronizes, and who has pledged all he is worth, and more, to get the liveries ready, which my lord has done him the honour to bespeak? When the great house tumbles down, these miserable wretches fall under it unnoticed: as they say in the old legends, before a man goes to the devil himself, he sends plenty of other souls thither.

The trickle-down theory of economics has it that it's good for rich people to get even richer because some of their wealth will trickle down, through their no doubt lavish spending, upon those who stand below them on the economic ladder. Notice that the metaphor is not that of a gushing waterfall but of a leaking tap: even the most optimistic endorsers of this concept do not picture very much real flow, as their language reveals. But everything in the human imagination and consequently in human life has both a positive and a negative version, and if the trickle-down theory of wealth is the positive, the negative is the trickle-down theory of debt. The debts that trickle down from large debtors may not in themselves be large, but they are large for those upon whom they trickle. Poor Mr. Raggles, from whom the Crawleys rent their house without ever paying for it, is utterly and completely ruined when the Crawley household falls apart and its members decamp.

Vanity Fair is named after the city of that same name in John Bunyan's *The Pilgrim's Progress*, where it stands not only for the "vanity of vanities, all is vanity" of the Book of Ecclesiastes, but especially for the realm of worldly goods, both material and spiritual, as well as for the state of mind in which absolutely everything is for sale. Bunyan's list of what's on offer in Vanity Fair is inclusive: "houses, lands, trades, places, honours, preferments, titles, countries, kingdoms, lusts, pleasures, and delights of all sorts, as whores, bawds, wives, husbands, children, masters, servants, lives, blood, bodies, souls, silver, gold, pearls, precious stones, and what not."

What not, indeed? Every human society sets a limit on what can be bought and sold, but in Bunyan's Vanity Fair there are no limits. Nevertheless, all who travel must pass through it, says Bunyan. It's a very sinister place, full of "jugglings, cheats, games, plays, fools, apes, knaves, and rogues," as well as "thefts, murders, adulteries, false-swearings, and that of a blood-red colour." In fact it's a suburb of Hell, and the journey through it ends with a horrific bout of torture and dismemberment. It's a vision born of shock—the shock caused by the old world of faith hitting the new one in which commerce is poised to become not only a king but an absolute monarch. Those loyal to the old order—an order in which there were virtues and loyalties, such as faith, hope, and charity, that were held to be above money—must have felt despairingly that Mammon was about to triumph, and Bunyan's dark strip-mall of a fair gives a shape to this feeling. The new world of money, in his eyes, is the City of Destruction, and the most important thing you can do is to make your way out of it as fast as possible.

By the mid-nineteenth century, however, that transition was far in the past. There was a certain amount of piety and Mrs. Grundyism around—a piano did not have legs, it had limbs, because "legs" was too suggestive, and a well-bred young lady never sat on a chair that a young man had just vacated, for fear that a seductive body heat might linger in the seat cushion—but an established churchman who knew what was good for him kept away from any thundering denunciations of the wickedness of riches. Thackeray's narrative voice is not that of the direct, urgent, outraged, and—some might say—naively trusting Bunyan, but the drawl of a bored and savvy worldling recording the way things are on this mundane social plane. His novel, he tells us, is a puppet show, and in a puppet show the characters are smaller than those observing them, and exist for our entertainment, not for our moral improvement. Thus Thackeray's *Vanity Fair* is a comic novel, or at least an ironic one: Rawdon Crawley and Becky Sharp get away with their acts of fraud and theft. In fact they get away literally, since each of them flees the field of their joint misdemeanours and ends up in a country that isn't England.

The tale of Becky Sharp and Rawdon Crawley is the comic version of Berne's "Try and Collect," but most of the nineteenth-century fictional treatments of debt are a lot darker. The theme of debt is so pervasive that it's difficult to choose examples. Shall we get born in a debtors' prison, like Dickens's Little Dorrit? Shall we follow the consequences of rashly contracted debts in *Uncle Tom's Cabin*, when human beings are sold to settle the account? Shall we plunge into huge financial ruin through *Dombey and Son*? Shall we move ahead several decades in time and ponder the sad fates of the two aspiring but eventually bankrupt and consequently dead writers in George Gissing's hard-edged novel of drudging scribery, *New Grub Street*?

Or shall we turn to debt as it impacts on women? We might start by investigating Flaubert's 1857 novel, *Madame Bovary*, the story of a provincial wife who takes to romantic love, extramarital sex, and overspending as an escape from boredom, but then poisons herself when her double life catches up with her and her unpaid creditor threatens to expose her. This book was put on trial for obscenity, and Flaubert defended it by brandishing Emma's hideous-looking corpse as an example of the book's inherent morality — the wages of sexual sin is arsenic, and not only does it kill you, it wrecks your looks — but that's a red herring. Emma isn't really punished for sex but for shopaholicism. Had she but learned double-entry bookkeeping and drawn up a budget, she could easily have gone on with her hobby of adultery forever — or at least until she got saggy — though she'd have done it in a more frugal manner.

Or perhaps we should cross the Atlantic and trace the pitiful career of Lily Bart in Edith Wharton's *House of Mirth*, who, had she known more about debt management, need not have ended up similarly self-poisoned. Rash Lily had not thought deeply enough about the principles of tit-for-tat: if a man lends you money and charges no interest, he's going to want payment of some other kind. Lily refuses to come across, and she also refuses to cynically cash in on the compromising letters of a false friend, and so there is no place for her in the worldly world: Lily Bart is pure as a lily, as her first name implies, but she's too pure to barter as her last name dictates. She's briefly up for sale in the marriage market, but she has no money so her price is not high, and she doesn't like the sleazy prospective bidders, and then her reputation gets unfairly besmirched, and who wants damaged goods?

Which leads us to reflect on the two nineteenth-century meanings of the word "ruin." For a nineteenth-century man, ruin was financial ruin — running up more debts than you could pay and then having the bailiffs and the foreclosers move in and grab your possessions. This would cause you to become shabby, after which former acquaintances would avoid you on the street. But for a nineteenth-century woman, ruin meant primarily sexual ruin — having sex, unwillingly or not, before marriage, or even being thought to have had it, which need not mean financial ruin at all, if a girl could turn things to her own account. To quote Thomas Hardy's wry poem "The Ruined Maid":

"O 'Melia, my dear, this does everything crown!
 Who could have supposed I should meet you in Town?
 And whence such fair garments, such prosperi-ty?"
"O didn't you know I'd been ruined?" said she.

"You left us in tatters, without shoes or socks,
 Tired of digging potatoes, and spudding up docks;
 And now you've gay bracelets and bright feathers three!"
"Yes: that's how we dress when we're ruined," said she.

"Your hands were like paws then, your face blue and bleak
 But now I'm bewitched by your delicate cheek,
 And your little gloves fit as on any la-dy!"
"We never do work when we're ruined," said she.

[...]

"I wish I had feathers, a fine sweeping gown,
 And a delicate face, and could strut about Town!"
"My dear, a raw country girl, such as you be,
 Cannot quite expect that. You ain't ruined," said she.

This poem points the way to the most exemplary novel for our purposes — a novel that combines debt with ruin of both kinds, the financial and the sexual. That novel is George Eliot's *The Mill on the Floss*, and it goes like this:

Two children, Maggie and Tom Tulliver, live beside the River Floss, at Dorlecote Mill — a water-wheel mill that grinds wheat into flour — where their father is the miller...

But here I must make a detour. For Maggie Tulliver is a miller's daughter, not a stationer's daughter or a plumber's daughter, and that makes a difference. So I'll say a few words about mills, because being a miller's daughter carries a heavy weight of mythic significance. As does being a miller. As, indeed, does being a mill.

Mills, millers, millers' daughters. I'll tackle them in that order.

Water-wheel mills are very old. In the West, they go back to Greek and Roman times, when, if anything was said about them, it tended to be good, since they replaced the labour of workers — slave workers, as a rule, like Samson with his eyes put out — and also that of animals. They were used by the Anglo-Saxons in England and were widespread in the Middle Ages. Somewhere along the line they began to pick up a dubious reputation. For one thing, they were a mechanical device, and for a superstitious peasant this made them objects not only of envy — *I wish I had one of those!* — but also of mistrust: *a thing that goes by itself must have some deviltry in it.* They might also inspire fear, of the what-if-it-goes-out-of-control or how-do-I-turn-it-off variety. For modern examples of this kind of fear, think about early robot movies, or else about your own first adventures with a Cuisinart.

There's a widespread folk motif about magic mills and their habit of not stopping. A poor peasant acquires a hand mill that goes by itself and grinds out anything you ask it to, and so he becomes wealthy; but someone else gets hold of it, and starts it grinding some desired substance — in *Grimm's Fairy Tales* it's porridge — and then can't turn it off, so the house and then the street fill up with porridge, dreadful thought. This plot is very close to the *Sorcerer's Apprentice* motif that you may last have glimpsed in Walt Disney's film *Fantasia*, with Mickey Mouse playing the apprentice and the unstoppable robot taking the form of a broom and a pail of water. Moral: beware of free lunches, because there aren't any: there's always a trick. Hermes is the god of tricks and lies and thieves and communication and commerce — everything that moves and flows — but he's also the god of mechanical devices, such as mills.

In the Andrew Lang *Blue Fairy Book* version of the tricky grinding hand mill that I read as a child, the peasant acquires the mill by going to Dead Man's Hall and doing a trade, whereby he gets the mill and the dead people get a ham. This makes sense in two ways: in folklore, the dead are always hungry, and newfangled mechanical devices — because of their uncanny natures — are likely to come from the other world, whatever that world may be called. The crafty peasant tells the mill to grind out gold, which it does — so much gold that his rich brother envies him. The rich brother manages to buy the mill and tells it to grind out some herrings; but he fails to ask how to turn it off, and is inundated with herrings. Finally, the mill is bought by a sea captain, who asks it to grind salt, because he trades in salt and this way he won't have to sail around all the time. But he, too, fails to find the Off switch, so he takes the infernal thing far out to sea and throws it overboard. It's down at the bottom of the ocean at this very moment, still grinding away, and that's why the sea is salt.

So now you know.

Next, you can ask yourself, Why is it *windmills* that the idealistic Don Quixote attacks in the belief that they are wicked giants? Why not, for instance, some other tall objects, such as trees or towers? But you already know the answer. The windmills go by themselves, and have a relentless juggernaut aspect to them, in addition to the evil repute that's attached to them just because they're mills. (In the wonderful opera *Don Quijote* by Cristóbal Halffter, mills are played by newspaper presses. Same idea, except now the mills are relentlessly grinding out news and rumours, both false and true.) Also, mills herald the coming Industrial Revolution, a thing Quixote intuits; and it, and everything it will bring with it, are bad news for a chivalric romantic like him, just as Vanity Fair is bad news for a religious romantic like John Bunyan.

William Blake recognized the same infernal qualities in mills. By the time he wrote his famous poem "Jerusalem," with its "dark Satanic mills," those mills were grinding out not only flour but fabric, and in the process gobbling up a lot of sickly wage slaves. But Blake's mills came with a ready-made Satanic reputation — one they'd inherited through the long hereditary line of mills. That line continued through the nineteenth century, spinning out such testaments to the Industrial Revolution as Elizabeth Gaskell's mill-town classic *Mary Barton*, and, in Canada, Frederick Philip Grove's tycoon-o-drama, *The Master of the Mill*.

Now for millers. When I was in grade three, we still had singing in school. Time to bring it back, now that the brain experts have told us it isn't a frill after all but a necessary aid in juvenile neural-pathway growth: short form, it makes kids smarter. At any rate, we did have singing back then, and we sang some odd songs. One of these was called "The Miller of Dee," and in the version I learned, it went like this:

There was a jolly miller once
Lived on the River Dee;
He worked and sang from morn to night,
No lark so blithe as he;
And this the burden of his song
Was ever wont to be —
I care for nobody, no, not I,
And nobody cares for me.

Why, I wonder, did anyone think this sociopathic role model was an appropriate one for us tiny songsters? There are some cleaned-up versions in which the miller cares for nobody *if* nobody cares for him, and in which he's made to stand as a model of sturdy English-yeoman financial independence; but I learned the one in which the miller doesn't give a hoot about anybody else, and this is most likely the original. In her article entitled "Mills and Millers in Old and New World Folksong," Jessica Banks tells us that millers in folklore are very often rendered as thieves and cheats who steal from the peasants by short-weighing and secretly diverting some of the flour they grind to their own use. There's a seventeenth-century proverb that goes: "Put a miller, a weaver, and a tailor together in a bag and shake them, and the first one that comes out will be a thief." In other words, all three professions are suspected of thievery. Why? Because, instead of growing something or making something — both of which result in tangibles, and are therefore understandable — they processed something: your grain into flour, your spun yarn into cloth, your woven cloth into clothing — and this value-added quality was hard to quantify. Also, some of the raw material could be pilfered.

It's the cheating kind of miller who turns up in Chaucer's "Reeve's Tale." This miller is wealthy and proud, and he manages to bag half a bushel of the meal that rightfully belongs to the two university clerks, or students, who've brought him the college's grain to be ground. But, as one of them says, there's a law that states "that if a man in one point be aggriev'd, Then in another he shall be reliev'd"; so they exact payment for their loss by foxily seducing both the miller's daughter and his wife, thus underlining the fact that with debts — especially debts that involve the wronged party's sense of honour — it's not always with money that the debt is discharged.

The other fact it underlines is that a miller's daughter is a dangerous thing to be, because you're likely to get the fallout from the miller's misdeeds. The ambiguous moral nature of mills and the sinister folkloric inheritance of millers are bound to attract trouble, and you may well find yourself right in the middle of that trouble.

There's a Grimm's tale called "The Girl Without Hands" that goes like this: a miller finds himself in financial difficulties, and finally he has nothing left but the mill and the apple tree that stands behind it. One day the miller meets a strange old man who says he'll make the miller rich in return for what is standing behind the mill. The miller thinks he means the apple tree and signs a written contract. (This story should be mandatory reading for all young law students as a warning about using vague language in legally binding documents.) But the strange man is Old Scratch — we readers knew that already, because who else tempts you to sign contracts of this almost-free-lunch kind? — and what is standing behind the mill is the miller's daughter.

The term of the contract is three years, and when the three years are up, the Devil appears to collect what's due, and wants to carry away the miller's daughter — who, in

Jungian terms, is a stand-in for the better side of the mill-er's soul. But she's a pious girl, and washes herself very clean, and since cleanliness is next to godliness the Devil has no power over her. He orders the miller to take away her washing water so she'll get dirty, but she cries so much on her hands that they stay very clean; so the Devil orders the hands cut off. But she similarly washes the stumps, so — three times lucky — the Devil has to go away, cheated of his bargain.

The rest of the story tells what happens to the miller's daughter when she travels out into the world, being understandably reluctant to stay with a father who's sold her to the Devil and cut off her hands. She's protected by an angel, who helps her eat a pear from the king's pear tree. This leads to marriage with the king, who makes her some silver hands. But the Devil still takes an interest in her, and tries to get her killed by the time-honoured device of exchanging the king's letters with letters of his own that falsely accuse her of having given birth to a monster — the usual sign that a girl has been wicked and unchaste — and order her to be put to death; so off she goes into the world again, supplied with a second guard-ian angel. Since "The Girl Without Hands" is a fairy tale, it all comes out right for her, with the king restored, and a lovely child; and she's been such a very good girl that her hands grow back as well.

George Eliot's *The Mill on the Floss* is not a fairy tale. Maggie and Tom Tulliver live at Dorlecote Mill with their father, Mr. Tulliver, the miller, who finds himself in financial difficulties. He doesn't meet the Devil and sign a contract with him, but he does the nineteenth-century equivalent: he puts himself and his family into danger because he's prone to pigheaded lawsuits. His lawsuits are about who owns the rights to the water in the River Floss: Tulliver is fighting such things as dams and irrigation projects that he's convinced will affect the flow of water to his mill. The lawyer acting for his opponents is Lawyer Wakem, and it's upon this lawyer that Tulliver focuses his fury and resentment.

Tulliver is an honest miller, Eliot tells us repeatedly; she has to tell us repeatedly, because his honesty goes against type. It's his adversary, Lawyer Wakem, who's the crafty, tricky miller of folklore; and he actually becomes a miller, in a way, since he eventually buys Tulliver's own mill. If Tulliver had been more dishonest, he might have grasped the rules of the game. As it is, he's merely angry, and ill-advised, and baffled by what he calls "the raskills." He loses his final lawsuit and has to pay heavy costs and damages, thus plunging himself and his family into debt, and the shock of losing everything causes him to have a stroke that renders him a temporary invalid. The mortgage on the mill is foreclosed, the household goods are seized and sold, and both Tom and Maggie — still teenagers — have to leave school and go out into the hard world of wage-earning to fend for themselves in the narrow provincial society that surrounds them.

This novel is usually read as the proto-feminist story of clever, impetuous, idealistic, passionate but thwarted

Maggie Tulliver, a woman born before her time — which it largely is. But what if we read it as the story of Mr. Tulliver's debt? For it's this debt that's the engine of the novel: it shoves the plot along, changes the mental states of the characters, and determines their scope of action. Without her father's debts, Maggie might have attracted a solid husband, but as it is, she's left penniless, which, in the nineteenth century, left her very vulnerable: not having money, then as now, severely limits one's choices, in matters of shopping and pair-bonding both. Maggie's a girl without hands, since in that era of limited opportunities for women there's not much honest work she can do to earn real money, and she's not skilled as a craftswoman: even her sewing is plain rather than fancy.

Lonely, feeling abandoned, and shut out from the good things of life, she becomes entangled in an emotional quadrangle — Philip Wakem, son of Lawyer Wakem, loves her; she loves her cousin Lucy's suitor Stephen; Stephen loves Maggie; Maggie feels loyal to Lucy. The upshot is that Maggie is wrongly suspected of sexual misconduct, like the girl with no hands. She's a pious girl, and renounces Stephen because she feels that to accept him and marry him would violate her Christian principles: such an act would be selfish, and would betray her cousin Lucy. But there's no guardian angel for Maggie: she's ruined. Almost everyone casts her off, including the minister who at first tries to defend her — his parishioners are starting to talk — and especially her beloved though hard-hearted and unforgiving brother, Tom. The mothers out there will be pleased to know that Mrs. Tulliver sticks by her, though the support of such a matron has nowhere near the authority it would have among a group of chimpanzees.

But meanwhile, unfortunate, bankrupted Mr. Tulliver has remained at Dorlecote Mill in the capacity of its manager. His boss is his enemy, Lawyer Wakem, who's bought the mill and hired Tulliver as a complicated act of revenge: "Prosperous men take a little vengeance now and then," says Eliot, "as they take a diversion, when it comes easily in their way, and is no hindrance to business; and such small unimpassioned revenges have an enormous effect in life, running through all degrees of pleasant infliction, blocking the fit men out of places, and blackening characters in unpremeditated talk."

It's the trickle-down theory of revenge, and Wakem is happy to participate in the process.

> ...it presented itself as a pleasure to him to do the very thing that would cause Mr. Tulliver the most deadly mortification, — and a pleasure of a complex kind, not made up of crude malice, but mingling with the relish of self-approbation. To see an enemy humiliated gives a certain contentment, but this is jejune compared with the highly blent satisfaction of seeing him humiliated by your benevolent action...That is a sort of revenge which falls into the scale of virtue, and Wakem was not without an intention of keeping that scale respectably filled.

Tulliver takes the job so he can stay in his beloved
ancestral home and provide a little security for his wife,
but he resents what Wakem is doing to him, and refuses to
forgive him, because forgiveness is "how Old Harry props
up the raskills." He makes Tom write in the family Bible
that neither Tulliver nor Tom will ever forgive Wakem,
and that he wishes evil may befall him. Maggie protests
that "it's wicked to curse and bear malice," and she's right;
it's especially ill-omened to use the Bible for the writing
paper in such a contract—for it is a contract, and Tom has
to sign it. But who's the other party to the contract? Is it
God? We doubt it. Tom has no compunctions about signing, however, being not of a naturally forgiving nature.

Tom secures a place in business, and with unrelenting
work and some clever trading on the side he earns
enough to pay off his father's debts. On the day the debts
are discharged, Mr. Tulliver encounters Lawyer Wakem,
who insults him again; but Tulliver now feels free to
throw over the job, and he gives Wakem a thrashing, "to
make things a bit more even in the world." Then he has
another stroke, and departs from the world while paying
tribute to the ancient notions of balance and justice: "'I
had my turn,' he says. 'I beat him. That was nothing but
fair. I never wanted anything but what was fair.'" Some
debts can't be discharged by money payments, and this
is one of them. Tulliver's been a debtor, but he also feels
himself a creditor: Wakem "owes" him for the shabby
treatment he's inflicted on Tulliver, and the debt must be
paid in pain and humiliation.

The conflict between Tulliver and Wakem is one we've seen before: the romantic and honest against the newfangled and mystifying and cynically exploitive — except that now the once-tricky and infernal mill and its miller are on the side of the old and naive, and the trickery now resides in the sharp practice of law. Power has moved from those who process material goods to those who process the contracts that govern them. Hermes — god of commerce, thieves, lies, contrivances, tricks, and mechanisms — has switched allegiances. And so it has remained to this day: we don't make "cheating miller" jokes any more, but how many "cheating lawyer" jokes do you know?

Things don't turn out well for the Tullivers, any more than they do for Don Quixote. Tulliver dies, and so — not long afterwards — do Tom and Maggie, who drown together in a flood, reconciled at the final moment. Like John Bunyan's Christian in *The Pilgrim's Progress* — a book much read by Tom and Maggie as children — they get their final reward by passing through the waters of death. As the saying goes, death pays all debts, which is true of the moral kind of debt anyway — the kind Maggie feels she owes to Lucy.

But Lawyer Wakem gets off, except for the thrashing. As I've said, it's not a fairy tale.

I BEGAN BY talking about debt as a story-of-my-life plot line, which is the approach Eric Berne takes in describing the variants of the life game of "Debtor."

But debt also exists as a real game — an old English parlour game. In fact, it's one of the games witnessed by the invisible Scrooge at his nephew's Christmas party. By no accident on the part of Dickens — for everything Scrooge is shown by the spirits must have an application to his own wicked life — this game is "Forfeits."

"Forfeits" has many variants, but here are the rules for perhaps the oldest and most complete form of it that we know about. The players sit in a circle, and one of them is selected to be the judge. Each player — including the judge — contributes a personal article. Behind the judge's back, one of these articles is selected and held up. The following verse is recited:

Heavy, heavy hangs over thy head.
What shall I do to redeem thee?

The judge — not knowing whose article it is — names some stunt or other that the owner of the article then has to perform. Much merriment is had at the absurdities that follow.

The real-life models on which this game is based are two in number. First and more benignly, there's the pawn-shop, in which the heavy thing hanging over the head is a debt that must be paid in order for the object to be redeemed. But "to deem" — the root of "redeem" — means not only to name in the sense of conferring identity, but also to judge: this meaning of it is related to the verb "to doom." And a forfeit means something lost through a crime or misdemeanour. So the second and more sinister model for the game of "Forfeits" is the condemning or dooming of a prisoner to death, and the heavy thing that hangs over the head is the executioner's axe, and the thing to be redeemed is a life.

There's nothing we human beings can imagine, including debt, that can't be turned into a game — something done for entertainment. And, in reverse, there are no games, however frivolous, that cannot also be played very seriously, and sometimes very unpleasantly. You'll know this yourself if you've ever played social bridge with a gang of white-haired ruthless ace-trumpers or watched any news items about cheerleaders' mothers trying to assassinate their daughters' rivals. Halfway between tiddlywinks and the Battle of Waterloo — between kids' games and war games — fall hockey and football and their ilk, in which the fans shouting "Kill!" are only partly joking. But when the play turns nasty in dead earnest, the game becomes what Eric Berne calls a "hard game." In hard games the stakes are high, the play is dirty, and the outcome may well be a puddle of gore on the floor.

It's to the hard games of debtor and creditor that I would like to turn in the next chapter, which will cover vengeance, crime, penalties, macroeconomics, billion-dollar defaults, and debt-driven revolutions. It's called, aptly enough, "The Shadow Side."

(FOUR)

THE SHADOW SIDE

I KNOW WHAT YOU'RE thinking: *Haven't you been shadowy enough already, what with all this talk about pawnshops of the soul, and sin-eating, and pacts with the Devil, and so forth? How much more shadowy can you get?* Quite a lot more, because it's shadowiest just before it gets even shadowier. But never mind: I'm saving the hopeful stuff for the very end of this book. Just like Pandora.

The question I'll try to address in this chapter is: What happens when people don't pay their debts? Or can't pay their debts? Or won't pay their debts? What then? And, an extension of this question: What if the debt is one that by its very nature cannot be repaid with money?

I STARTED THINKING about the subject of debt for a number of reasons, but among them was my puzzlement over a turn of phrase — one you don't hear very often any more, although you still do hear it. "He's paid his debt to society," it used to be said. "Crime does not pay," we also used to say, optimistically thinking this meant that crime does not ultimately reward the criminal; whereas it might mean instead — pessimistically — that Crime skips town and stiffs you for his bills, the rotten deadbeat.

In the lurid, trashy 1940s crime comics I read as a kid, crime *didn't* pay. In these moral though gruesome narratives, the criminals committed many noir deeds, usually in the glare of a single unshaded light bulb or two cone-shaped car headlights, but they always got caught in the end. "The jig's up," someone would say, leading to more puzzlement for me — what was a jig? — was it an Irish dance, and if so, what did its being up or down signify? — or else they got splattered against a wall in a burst of red and yellow machine-gun fire, emitting cries of "Arrgh." However, if arrested rather than terminated, they were made to pay in another sense of the term: they had to do something called "paying for their crimes."

This phrase suggests a crime supermarket in which you can browse among the various crimes on offer and select those you want to do, take them to the checkout counter, render your cash or credit card — more for bigger crimes, less for smaller ones — and then merrily go out and commit them. The equivalent of this crime supermarket has actually existed in the past — the Catholic Church once sold indulgences, whereby you paid after completing the bad act, rather than before; and the same sort of thing is still available under various names — Hells Angels, the Mafia, and many another crime-for-hire enterprise. I'm told the terms are half down and half on delivery. But that isn't what paying for your crimes is usually thought to mean.

Similarly, "paying your debt to society" didn't often mean a fine. Instead it meant an execution or a jail term. Let's ponder this in the light of everything we've said about the debtor and the creditor as joined-at-the-hip twins balanced on the two sides of a scale, with equilibrium arriving when all debts are paid. If the person being executed or jailed is the debtor who's thought to owe something to somebody, and if that creditor is society, in what way does society benefit from the execution or the incarceration? It certainly doesn't profit financially, since it costs a bundle to put people on trial and then lock them up, or cut off their heads, or disembowel them, or burn them at the stake, or electrify them so that smoke comes out of their ears, and so forth. So there must be some other kind of payment intended.

If we were still operating on a strict Mosaic eye-for-an-eye repayment scheme, there would be some sense to the execution part — that is, if the individual being executed had murdered someone. One dead body would result in another dead body, thus balancing the scales. But doing time in jail isn't an obvious equivalent of anything — that's why the jail-time verdicts for any given crime vary so widely from era to era and from place to place — and the material benefit to society is not only zero, it's considerably less than zero, because it's not the jailed criminal who's actually paying for anything, it's the taxpayer. And the two commonly heard justifications for locking people up — as a deterrent to other would-be crime committers, and as a way of accomplishing the moral improvement of the locked-up person — don't appear to work out very well in money terms. Education is a better and cheaper deterrent, community service a better and cheaper moral improver.

Alas, the kind of payment actually meant by "paying for your crimes" really amounts to vengeance. So the debit side — the crime itself, and the ruination it may have caused to others — and the credit side — the self-righteous gloating, the feeling that the scum-bucket is getting a well-deserved comeuppance — can't really be translated into cash equivalents at all. Similarly, some debts can never be money debts: they're debts of honour. With these, it's felt that other forms of payment must be exacted, and these other forms most often have to do with the infliction of nasty blunt- or sharp-implement procedures on other people's bodies. "Hamlet, remember," says the ghost of Hamlet's father, but he doesn't mean that Hamlet should go to Claudius and say, "So, you murdered my dad, that'll be a thousand ducats." He means that the accounts will not be balanced until Claudius is dead, not of old age but of revenge at the hand of Hamlet.

Revenge is a fascinating topic — fascinating to all those who have ever kicked their sibling under the table and received a harder kick in return, or who have thrown a snowball and received back a rock — and it's one I'm sure you're longing to hear about, with examples. For instance, the jilted girlfriend who snuck into her ex's flat and cut heart-shaped holes in his expensive designer ties and smeared anchovy paste on his bedroom curtains; or the discarded boyfriend who had a dozen large black-ribboned funeral wreaths sent to his one-time lover, plus the bill for them; or, even worse, the fellow who called up the police and said there was a dead body in his ex's house, but they were in denial over there and would pretend there wasn't one, so the police would need a search warrant; or — far from such children's games played in polite Canadian society — the mangled corpses that turn up on people's doorsteps when there's an old-time blood feud going on in a country where these rituals are still obligatory. Such things cannot be quantified — they're evaluated subjectively, like art — so there's no way of telling whether any given revenge item has in fact evened the scales. Revenge, therefore, can quickly turn into a long chain reaction of revenges, each one worse than the last.

But I'll hold the revenge segment till later. Not only is revenge a dish best served cold, but it will take us on a shadowy Tunnel of Horrors ride into the darker and more bone-strewn corners of the human psyche; and such experiences ought to be left until the finale. First, we'll go on a relatively jolly tour of the lighter suburbs of Shadowland: that is, the various consequences that can flow from the nonpayment of debts that are strictly financial in nature.

WHAT HAPPENS IF you owe a legitimate money debt and you don't pay it? This can overlap with "can't pay" or "won't pay," as in the expression French parents use with their children: "Tu ne peux pas, ou tu ne veux pas?" *You can't, or you won't?* Whichever it is, different societies have instituted numerous hammers and tongs and kicks and torments to make the debtor cough up: for without her sword, or at least the wherewithal to give you a hefty slap on the wrist, the Goddess of Justice is powerless.

In the past there have been many severe penalties for nonpayment, from debt slavery to seizure of assets. In England, from the seventeenth century until the early nineteenth, your creditor could have you arrested and accused of concealing your wealth, and then have you thrown into an overcrowded, dank, and filthy debtors' prison, where you had to languish either until you paid up or until someone bailed you out by paying up for you. While in there, you had to cover the costs of your own food and lodging — a cruel twist, considering that you'd been incarcerated for not having any money in the first place. So unless someone came to your rescue, you were likely to starve and freeze to death. The redoubtable eighteenth-century writer Doctor Samuel Johnson had this to say about debtors' prisons:

> It is vain to continue an institution which experience shows to be ineffectual. We have now imprisoned one generation of debtors after another, but we do not find that their numbers lessen. We have now learned, that rashness and imprudence will not be deterred from taking credit: let us try whether fraud and avarice may be more easily restrained from giving it.... Those who

made the laws have apparently supposed, that every deficiency of payment is a crime of the debtor. But the truth is, that the creditor always shares the act, and often more than shares the guilt, of improper trust. It seldom happens that any man imprisons another but for debts which he suffered to be contracted in hope of advantage to himself, and for bargains in which proportioned his own profit to his own opinion of the hazard: and there is no reason, why one should punish the other for a contract in which both concurred.

In other words, both the borrower and the lender were to blame if their arrangement didn't work out: the former for endangering his security by borrowing, the latter for seeking to make a profit — assumed to be an excessive profit — from the desperation or the excessive risk-taking of the borrower. Their contract had been entered into out of self-interest on both sides, and the bad judgement and greediness of both were therefore to blame for its failure. It is more than possible that Dr. Johnson took such a lenient view of imprisoned debtors because he'd come so very close to being one himself.

It was often the case that the English debtor's family moved into the prison with him, and the wife and children went out to work in order to pay for the whole family's room and board. This is fairly close to the Code of Hammurabi of four thousand years before, whereby you could sell your wife and kids to pay off your debts. It's also fairly close to the bonded child labourers in India today, estimated by Human Rights Watch to be fifteen million in number, who work long, hard hours to pay off debts incurred by their parents — parents who often have no other way of trying to pay back the money. But in nineteenth-century England, the word for this kind of child-and-family labour was not "slavery." That word was reserved for another form of slavery, whereby somebody claimed to own another person completely. Yet the child debt labourers were, and are, just as unfree.

Charles Dickens's father was thrown into the Marshalsea debtors' prison, and the twelve-year-old Charles was pulled out of school and sent to work in a blacking factory — a despair-filled experience that darkened his whole life and came back in dreams to haunt him. Nonchalant wastrels, charming bankrupts, no-good scroungers, and despairing debt prisoners occur throughout his work, and the Scroogy side of Scrooge's nature comes from Dickens himself — he was openly generous in many ways but also very tight with a penny, so afraid was he of following in the footsteps of his improvident father.

Dickens's best-known fictional bankrupt is Mr. Micawber, from *David Copperfield* — said to be modelled on Dickens Senior — who's always waiting for "something to turn up," but who, when it does turn up, spends it on drink. Micawber's recipe for happiness is often quoted. When young David goes to visit him in the debtors' prison, he cries a lot, and then, says David, "He solemnly conjured me, I remember, to take warning by his fate; and to observe that if a man had twenty pounds a-year for his income, and spent nineteen pounds nineteen shillings and sixpence, he would be happy, but that if he spent twenty pounds one he would be miserable." This is said to have been a direct quote from Dickens Senior.

However, the remainder of Mr. Micawber's moralizing-speech paragraph is *not* often quoted: "After which he borrowed a shilling of me for porter, gave me a written order on Mrs. Micawber for the amount, and put away his pocket-handkerchief, and cheered up." Micawber is a man who's painted himself into a corner with no way out of it that he can see, and so he simply enjoys the corner. Many of the debtors Dickens portrays are conscious of their humiliation and disgrace, but not Mr. Micawber. The old blues song "Been Down So Long It Seems Like Up to Me" could have been sung by him. He even mooches off other debtors, so shameless a character is he. He's far from being honest and responsible and conscientious, and he's a great humbug — his tears are mostly acting; but the reader half admires him for his jaunty ability to shrug off his burdens, and so, in a way, does Dickens. At least Mr. Micawber is not malicious. He means no harm, although he causes it.

Debtors' prisons were largely an Old World phenomenon. Urban overcrowding there made labour cheap, but in early and rapidly developing North America there was such a demand for able-bodied workers that keeping people in jail because they hadn't paid their bills made no economic sense at all. Instead, such debtors were forced to become indentured labourers — workers bound to serve a specified employer until the debt was paid off. "Community service" is the closest thing to this now, though it's not often used as a substitute for nonpayment of debt. In Western societies, we do still jail people for not paying up, most often in cases of failure to provide child support; even so, the charge is likely to be contempt of court. It's punishment for a perceived attitude—"You won't pay"—rather than lack of funds—"You can't pay."

Apart from that, the things that can happen to you in North America nowadays if you don't pay your debts are so non-life-threatening as to make little impression on the extravagant borrower. I'm told that university students tell tales about their ballooning student loans with rueful grins rather than with floods of despairing tears. Everyone's in debt—so what? That's the way it is, and how else are they supposed to get through school? As for paying it all off, they'll think about that later.

A friend of mine—this was back in the 1970s—was on the receiving end of one of those injudicious mailings that the newly born credit card companies went in for in those days. They'd send you a card in the mail, no questions asked, and they sent my friend one, and he quickly spent the limit. There followed a lively game of "Try and Collect." He'd pay a small amount every month—five dollars and thirty-two cents, or some paltry and annoying sum like that. And the credit card company did become annoyed, and turned the account over to a collections agency. Then my friend started getting tirades over the phone. This was back in the days before the invention of the little window that showed you who was calling.

"Excuse me," my friend would say to the collection caller. "I understand why you have to call me, but I object to your tone of voice. There is no need for you to be rude. If it weren't for people like me, people like you wouldn't have a job. So call, by all means, but please be polite about it."

"Oh. All right," said the collections agency caller, seeing the logic of the position. And, this being Canada, he was indeed polite from then on.

Nowadays, those drowning in debt have a resource that wasn't always available in the past: they can declare personal bankruptcy and more or less walk away from the whole mess. There are agencies that will help you do this, for a cut. "Settle for less than you owe," coo the subway advertisements. True, there are drawbacks — your credit rating will be affected, and you'll lose some of your flashier toys — but you won't be thrown into a cold, dark dungeon where you'll have to live on cheese rinds and mouldering bread, and where the other prisoners will steal your silk handkerchief and your boots and your cuff buttons. Not usually. Not here. Not yet.

SO FAR WE'VE been talking about what might legitimately be done to you for nonpayment of debts that were contracted legally. But what if the debt itself has been arranged in some shady nook outside the borders of the law? What, for instance, if the debtor has borrowed the money from a Mafia loan shark? Then the pressures brought to bear may be of quite a different order.

My chief source of information on such matters is the inimitable Elmore Leonard. In his crime novel *Get Shorty*, his anti-hero, Chili Palmer, is employed as a skip tracer for the Mafia, and he's chasing around after a compulsive small-time gambler who's playing a hard but stupid game of "Try and Collect." Chili has this to say about the techniques of loan sharks:

> A guy comes to see you, it doesn't matter how much he wants or why he needs it, you say to him up front before you give him a dime, "You sure you want to take this money? You're not gonna put up your house or sign any papers. What you're gonna give me is your word you'll pay it back so much a week with interest."... If the guy hesitates at all, "Well. I'm pretty sure I can"— says anything like that, I tell him, "No, I'm advising you now, don't take the fuckin' money." The guy will beg for it, take an oath on his kids he'll pay you on time. You know he's desperate or he wouldn't be borrowing shylock money in the first place. So you tell him, "Okay, but you miss even one payment you're gonna be sorry you ever came here." You never tell the guy what could happen to him. Let him use his imagination, he'll think of something worse.

Later, Chili adds a gloss: "You have to understand the loan shark's in business the same as everyone else. He isn't in it looking for a chance to hurt people. He's in it to make money." But the corollary is that if the loan shark doesn't make his money, then he is going to hurt people. In the shadowland of borrowing and lending, just as there are no limits set to the nature and size of the debt, so there are no limits set to the nature and grisliness of the penalty for nonpayment. As Chili says, there's always something worse.

SO FAR WE'VE been confining our focus to the individual debtor. The civilian debtor, the common-or-garden variety of debtor, the pedestrian debtor; the debtor without an army. But what happens if we enlarge the screen? What if the borrower is — for instance — a king, or an emperor, or a Renaissance duke, or a Genghis-Khan- or Attila-the-Hun-style warlord, or a modern government, democratic or not? Then things get even worse than Chili Palmer's "something worse"; for, like hurricanes, volcanic eruptions, and tidal waves, big debts can make history and rearrange the landscape.

In *The Prince* — his instructive sixteenth-century treatise on how to govern with an iron fist in a very ornate and perfumed velvet glove — Niccolò Machiavelli lays such matters right out on the table with chilling but hard-to-refute logic. What leaders or would-be leaders most want and need to do, he says, is to gain, expand, and consolidate power. To do this, they need followers and subjects — in our day, for democracies, read "party members" and "taxpayers." They can acquire their territory by inheritance, by force of conquest, or by guile and treachery; but in any case they will need an army, or a national police force — anyway, some folks with weaponry — and, to feed and equip their army, they will need money.

They can pay the army either by conquering more territory and going in for looting and pillaging — thus spending other people's wealth — or by spending wealth of their own that they might already have, or by taxing their subjects. But if they tax their subjects too much — "too much" probably being the point past which the subject's inner child is screaming "That's not fair!" for more than twelve hours a day — they inspire hatred and invite rebellion. On the other hand, if they tax their subjects *really* too much, so that widespread poverty and starvation result, the subjects may be too malnourished and weak and feeble to rebel; in addition to which, they will lose the incentive and the strength to do any productive labour. But on yet another hand, if things go that far, the subjects may feel they have nothing to lose by rebelling. It's a fine calculation.

A nice way of putting the whole matter of taxation is that governments borrow from the people — sometimes they really do borrow, in the form of bond issues — and then they owe their people a debt that should be repaid in services rendered. Even Machiavelli says that the Prince should try to improve the lot of his subjects, if possible. (What "if possible" seems to mean is "If there's possibly any money left over from the expense of all the wars I intend to wage.") What the subjects want is to have the services without paying the taxes, and what the rulers want is to have the taxes without rendering the services — these conflicting wants appear to be a constant in human history, ever since there have been food surpluses and social hierarchies, and armies, and taxes — so there's always bound to be some grumbling.

Nevertheless, you can float many a hefty tax scheme on the back of a righteous-sounding and energizing war. Wars focus the attention; people don't want to feel or even appear disloyal at such times. Scare them with the thought that they themselves may be looted and pillaged by bands of slavering, subhuman barbarians who will roast and eat their children and ravish and eviscerate their women — don't laugh, it's happened — and they'll fork over with remarkable docility, if not eagerness. Just to remind you: the income tax was begun in Great Britain in 1799, to finance the Napoleonic Wars. In the United States, it began in 1862, to support the Civil War. In Canada, in 1917, incomes were first taxed as a temporary measure to finance the First World War. And taxes are like zebra mussels: once they've been introduced, they're very hard to get rid of. The wars the income taxes were meant to pay for have come and gone, but the income taxes themselves persist. Oh well, it's better than a tax on windows, or beards, or bachelors, all of which have also had their day.

It's remarkable how often the assumed debt of services in return for the citizen's tax dollar is forgotten by governments at large. And once the money's been spent, the people have no means of recovering the sums they've been forced to lend, since they aren't the ones with the army. In a democracy, you can depose an unpopular leader by voting for somebody else. In a tyranny, you can risk an armed coup or a popular uprising. But in either system, even if you win the election or the coup or the uprising, you'll still be out of pocket. In the very worst scenario, your children will still be starving and/or uneducated, your water purification plant will still be unbuilt, your tax money will be in a numbered bank account in Switzerland, and your ex-tyrant will be sunning himself on the Riviera, surrounded by a high wall and a posse of expensive bodyguards. Or, in a democracy, your money will have vanished up the sleeves of your ex-leader's political cronies via a bouquet of untendered and overpriced contracts, and that ex-leader will be warming the seat cushions of half a dozen grateful boards of directors, far from the madding journalists. On the other hand, if things get chaotic enough and riots are afoot, you might be able to parade through the streets with somebody's head on a stick, shouting, "The jig is up!" But though satisfying as an act of revenge, this is a temporary thrill, and it still won't restore your vanished money.

A jig, by the way — and I know you've been wondering — doesn't only mean a form of Irish dancing. It can also mean a game or trick or ingenious mechanism. Some tax systems are jigs, in this sense of the word. They are ingenious mechanisms for extracting more money than the extractor ever intends to pay back in the form of services rendered.

THERE ARE TWO kinds of taxation systems: ones that are resented, and ones that are *really* resented. The Roman Empire, during its expansionist phase — the first century B.C.E. — had one of the really resented kind, since it went in for tax farming to support its ongoing military ventures. Here's how the tax farming worked. The leaders would set a tax quota for an entire community, and local tax collectors would bid on the right to pay that amount or more to Rome — the highest bidder being the winner. The tax collector would pay the state up front, and would then have the right to grind the money out of the local population.

Needless to say, his goal would be to collect more than he'd actually paid to Rome and then keep the difference for himself. Fortunes were made through all kinds of cheats and stratagems — taking goods instead of cash while undervaluing them, then selling the goods at a profit; cornering the grain market, thus creating scarcity, then selling back to the population at exorbitant prices what you'd squeezed out of them as taxes, and so forth. That this was a highly corrupt system goes without saying. Some historians have listed it as one of the causes for the collapse of the Roman Empire: grind the peasants too much and they cease to yield. It's like any predator-prey pyramid: if there are no more little fish, the population of big fish collapses. Lest you think that Rome was the only outfit ever to do this, think again. The Ming Dynasty in China undermined itself in much the same way; so did the Ottoman Empire; and so did the French monarchy before Louis the Sixteenth.

The name for the Roman tax collectors was *publicani* — which gives us that intriguing phrase in the New Testament, "publicans and sinners." I used to think that the publicans were the men who ran the pubs, and that their publicanism had something to do with the winebibbers usually mentioned in the same breath. Jesus of Nazareth had a habit of hanging out with all three kinds of badly behaved people — publicans, sinners, and winebibbers — and now that I've told you about the tax farming, you can understand why the palship of the *publicani*, in particular, would have been viewed by Jesus' compatriots as colouring really, really far outside the moral box.

The exploitative Roman tax-farming system also explains why the opponents of Jesus asked him whether it was sinful to pay taxes to Rome, thus giving rise to his well-known reply: "Render unto Caesar the things that are Caesar's, and unto God the things that are God's." This answer was a clever way of getting out of a trap, the trap being that if you said Yes to paying the Roman taxes you endorsed a peasant-grinding tax system, but if you said No to paying them you'd be charged with sedition by the Roman tyrants — but it's caused some head-scratching ever since. Is money in general a thing of Caesar's? Did

Jesus mean, *Cheat the taxman*? In addition to which, many governments have gone out of their way to give the impression that God and they are firmly in cahoots, so that paying them is the same as paying God. Or almost the same. Or as close as maybe. Just take a look at what governments write on their money, even today. In Canada, it's *Elizabeth D.G. Regina*, short for *Dei Gratia Regina* — Queen by the Grace of God. In Britain, it's a longer inscription that adds initials meaning "Defender of the Faith." And in America, there's the motto "In God We Trust"—which, when I was in high school, gave rise to a joke: "In God we trust, all others pay cash." But there's a distinct advantage to having "God" written on your government's money: it appears to give the currency a divine imprimatur.

Resentment over heavy taxation has given rise to a great many rebellions over the centuries. To clarify terms: if your rebellion succeeds, it's called a "revolution." Otherwise it's just a rebellion. The heavy taxes that were so resented very often had to do with wars. Thus the Hundred Years' War between England and France inspired a rebellion in France in 1358 called "the Jacquerie"—a term that was picked up later during the French Revolution — and it also inspired a rebellion in England in 1381 that was kicked off by a poll tax levied to raise war funds. Among the grievances was a move made by the nobility to restore the feudal system, whereby peasants were bound to the land and owed unpaid labour to their lords — in effect, a sort of serfdom. This system had been eroded by the Black Death, which, by killing off half the population of Europe, had created a shortage of workers, thus upping the standard minimum wage and increasing peasant bargaining power. The moral: even the Black Death was good for something.

The 1381 English rebellion was led by a yeoman called Wat Tyler, and one of the participants was a priest named John Ball, who preached a sermon containing the famous rhyme, "When Adam delved and Eve span / Who was then the gentleman?" The password among the rebels was "John the Miller grinds small, small, small," to which the right answer was "And the king's son of heaven shall pay for all." I've come across no definitive interpretation of this, but I would take the line about the miller grinding small to be a reference to the often quoted ancient Greek saying, "The mills of the gods grind slowly, but they grind exceeding small," meaning "Retribution may be slow in coming, but when it does come, the wicked will be crushed to dust." The response, "And the king's son of heaven shall pay for all" meant, I expect, that if the rebels had to kill a few people while doing the small grinding of their enemies, they'd be forgiven for it in the afterlife — their debt of sin having been paid for by the sacrificial blood of Christ. They did kill some people before being defeated and executed in horrible ways, but they mainly assaulted the tax collectors and burnt their records. Without memory there is no debt, and a written record is a form of memory; and whenever there's been a tax-and-debt-inspired uprising, one of the prime targets has been the tax and debt records. The principle at work was, *If you can't prove it, I don't owe it.*

The American Revolution was another revolt that came about as the result of a tax perceived as unjust — imposed this time to pay for a war that had already taken place. The war was the Seven Years' War between England and France, and it included the capture of Quebec in 1759. Had Quebec not fallen, there wouldn't have been any American Revolution, as the colonists of that time couldn't have afforded their own standing army to defend themselves against the French. Once New France was in the hands of the British, however, the American colonists were free to revolt, which they promptly did. You remember what they said on that occasion: "No taxation without representation." Yes, it was a tax war.

To get back at England for their bad taste in having won the Seven Years' War, the absolute monarchy of France supported the American revolutionaries, thus endorsing a model of anti-monarchist action, which was reckless of them. Also they spent too much money supporting the Americans, so they upped the taxes on their already threadbare population. There was a protest movement, featuring — among others — some non-aristocratic people known as the *sans culottes*. I used to think this meant they were so poor that they didn't have any pants, but in fact it meant they didn't have any knee breeches — these being the fashion choice of the aristocracy. Such sartorial distinctions became very important during the ensuing French Revolution of 1789, as they do during all revolutions. After the fall of the Bastille there were massive peasant uprisings and burnings of the chateaux of all those with *culottes*, and the tax and debt records were again among the first things to be destroyed.

This pattern is not a thing of the past. Burma in 1930, Vietnam — also in 1930 — and the Philippines in 1935 all saw anti-colonial rebellions focused on harsh taxes imposed by imperialist powers who were using the funds for the Machiavellian goals of gaining, expanding, and consolidating their own power. We think of the Hungarian uprising of 1956 as being some sort of spontaneous blow struck for democracy, but in fact it, too, was driven on by harsh taxation that can be traced to the U.S.S.R., which was involved in the Cold War arms race at the time. In all of these, one of the primary goals of the rebels was to destroy the tax and debt records. This was a very graphic way of wiping the slate clean.

If you're a king, prince, tyrant, or democratic government and you want to do some war waging but don't want to inspire a tax revolt by grinding the peasants too small, you can get hold of the money in other ways, such as borrowing it. There are three sources for such non-tax loans: (1) your own subjects, to whom you can sell war bonds; (2) the moneylenders within your own country; (3) the governments or financial institutions of other countries. If you borrow too much from other countries, you'll sooner or later find yourself constrained in your sphere of power-expanding-and-consolidating action, because if that other country doesn't like what you're doing they can pull their financial support as lenders. But then, you can always threaten to default on your already-large loans and they will be stuck with a deficit. So it's still a case of debtor and creditor joined at the hip.

(I need not whisper, "America and China at the present moment." But I'll whisper it anyway, adding simply: as Machiavelli said, it's terrible policy for a leader to plunge his country severely into debt. It results in a loss of power and influence — often the very things that the leader waged the expensive war to gain. Looting and pillaging are all very well, but do the math first. Just remember: total loot-and-pillage profit, minus the time it takes, multiplied by cost-per-war-minute, equals either the red or the black. If it's the red, take Mr. Micawber's advice and don't do it.)

However, if the moneylenders are not some other country but are situated within your own kingdom, and you've borrowed what you feel is too much money from them, you can play a very dirty trick. This dirty trick has indeed been played, and quite often. It's called "Kill the Creditors." (Please don't try this at your local bank.)

Consider, for instance, the sad fate of the Knights Templar. They were a religious order of fighting knights who'd amassed a great store of capital through gifts given to them by the pious, as well as through various treasures they'd acquired during the Crusades, and they acted as Europe's major moneylenders — to kings as well as to others — for more than two centuries. It was unlawful for Christians to charge "usury" for the use of money, but it wasn't unlawful for them to charge "rent" for the use of land, so the Templars charged so-called "rent" for the use of money, which you paid at the same time you got the loan, rather than after you'd used it. But you still had to pay the principal amount back at the stipulated time. This could be a problem for those who'd borrowed the money, as it still is today.

In 1307, Philip the Fourth of France found he owed a cumbersome lot of money to the Templars. With the aid of the Pope and of torture, he accused them — falsely — of heretical and sacrilegious activities and had them rounded up and burned at the stake. As if by magic, his debts disappeared. (So did the vast wealth of the Templars, which has never been adequately accounted for since.)

Philip was basing his behaviour on a pre-existing and popular "Kill the Creditors" model, which might be called "Kill the Jewish Creditors." It was against the Christian religion at that time to charge interest for loans, but it wasn't against the Jewish religion for Jews to charge interest to non-Jews; and since in most countries where they lived Jews were forbidden to be landholders — land being considered the real source of wealth — they were forced into the profession of moneylending, for which they were then resented and despised. But the money they made by moneylending was in return frequently taxed by the kings. So a handy but dangerously symbiotic relationship came into being: the Jews made money by lending money, and the kings made money by taxing the money the Jews made. The borrowers might be the kings themselves, or they might be the nobles — nobles who, in true Machiavellian fashion, were trying to build up their own power and influence in order to become kings, or possibly king-makers, or king-breakers — in any case, something farther up the ladder; and climbing that ladder cost money. Which they often borrowed from the Jews.

This mix of money, kings, nobles, and Jews was volatile, and resulted in numerous outbreaks of "Kill the Jewish Creditors," driven on by an ever-ready and convenient anti-Semitism. I'll confine my examples to England, though there are many other such stories from all over Europe. For instance: at York, in 1190, a group of noblemen who owed a lot of money to Jewish moneylenders got up a mob and went after the Jewish population. The same device was used as for the Templars, namely, accusations of a religious nature. The Jews had been under the protection of Richard the First, but he'd gone off to the Crusades. There was a massacre, and you can predict what happened next: the records of the debts were burned. But Richard had depended on the Jews to finance — guess what — his war effort; so he was annoyed. He instituted a system of duplicate records, and then proceeded to tax the Jews even more than he had before.

In the thirteenth century, things got even worse for the Jews in England, with massacres at frequent intervals; in addition to which, various unsustainable taxes were levied on them by the king. Understandably, they asked to leave England in 1255, but Henry the Third refused this request, because the Jews were a convenient source of revenue for him; so convenient, indeed, that he declared them royal property, as if they were parks. But successive legal changes that restricted their activities even further — barring them from moneylending but not opening up much else — rendered them poor, and in 1290 they were expelled from England, which thus became the first country to do such a thing.

Lest you think that this pattern has occurred only in connection with Jewish moneylenders and the Knights Templar, let me remind you of Idi Amin's expulsion of the East Indians from Uganda in 1972 — the East Indians were highly represented in the banking business — and of the treatment of the ethnic Chinese in Vietnam in the 1970s, including their expulsion. Whenever you have an out-group to whom an in-group owes a lot of money, "Kill the Creditors" remains an available though morally repugnant way of cancelling your debts. Note: you need not resort to murder as such. If you make people run away very fast, they'll leave all their stuff behind, and then you can grab it. And burn the debt records: that goes without saying.

You'll notice I got through this part without mentioning the Nazis. The point being that I didn't have to. For they have not been alone.

NOW WE ARE entering the shadowiest location in our tour of the shadow side of debt. Yes: we are approaching the Land of Revenge, the place where money can't buy you out of a debt of honour. At this point I'd like to go back to the primate sense of fairness with which I began this book. You'll recall that the monkeys in the experiment I described were quite happy to trade pebbles for slices of cucumber until one monkey was given a more cherished grape instead, whereupon most of the monkeys stopped trading. There's also an experiment in which two monkeys were able to obtain a coveted food item by pulling together on a rope — neither one being able to accomplish this task solo. But the food was then available to only one of them. If this one refused to share, the second monkey would in future retaliate by refusing to pull on the rope. He preferred to punish the selfish monkey rather than take a chance at getting some food himself.

You know the feeling. Everyone knows it. Could it be that the revenge module is very ancient and thus deeply embedded in us? Some cultures encourage its expression more than others do, but it seems to be omnipresent. Simply telling people they ought not to feel vengeful because it isn't nice will not usually work.

"Economic man" is a creature beloved of economists, who like to believe we're motivated purely by economic considerations. If that were true, the world would be not necessarily a better but a very different place. Money — like the monkeys' pebbles — is simply a medium of exchange. It can be changed into all sorts of other things, including lives. Sometimes it's been used as payment for a death you may have caused — of a cow, a horse, or a person. Sometimes it's been used to pay for a death you may want caused, and sometimes to keep a death from happening—in these last two cases we refer to it as "blood money." But sometimes these money equations just won't suffice: only the blood will do.

In Charles Dickens's novel about the French Revolution, *A Tale of Two Cities,* the much-wronged Madame Defarge spends the time leading up to the Terror keeping a knitted record of all those whose heads must fall once the storm breaks. As her husband says, "It would be easier for the weakest poltroon that lives, to erase himself from existence, than to erase one letter of his name or crimes from the knitted register of Madame Defarge." Her knitting recalls the Greek Fates—those three sisters who spun out men's destinies, then snipped off their threads—but it's also a sinister version of the debt records we've been talking about; and when the guillotine is up and running, Madame Defarge goes to all the executions and counts the heads, and unknits the names of the victims, because their "forfeit" has been paid in blood.

Beside Madame Defarge sits another of the knitting women, whose nickname is "The Vengeance." She's a stand-in for the presiding deities of the Revolution, who are our old acquaintances the goddess Nemesis—or Retribution—and the red-eyed, relentless Furies. When the more balanced goddess, Justice, with her blindfold and her scales loses control, these more ancient and more bloodthirsty goddesses come rampaging in.

I'll pause here to consider the word "revenge," which, according to the *Oxford English Dictionary,* is derived from the Latin *revindicare*. And *revindicare* is derived from *vindicare*, which means to justify or rescue or liberate or emancipate, as in liberating a slave. Thus, to revenge yourself upon someone is to reliberate yourself, because before doing the revenge, you aren't free. What holds you in thrall? Your obsession with your own hatred of the other: your own vengefulness. You feel that you can't shake free of it except through the act of revenge. The score that needs to be settled is a psychic score, and the kind of debt that can't be paid with money is a psychic debt. It's a wound to the soul.

Revengers and those they wish to kill or punish are like creditors and debtors. They come in pairs. They're joined at the hip. And it's just a short step from here to the Jungian theory of the Shadow.

In narratives involving irrational and obsessive hatred, especially of some person or group one doesn't really know very well, such hatred—say the Jungians—is the mark of a person who has not come to terms with his or her own Shadow. The Shadow is our dark side, the repository of everything in us we're ashamed of and would rather not acknowledge, and also of those qualities we profess to despise but would in fact like to possess. If we haven't acknowledged those things about ourselves, we're likely to project them onto somebody else or some other group, and to develop an irrational hatred toward that person or group. In fiction, the Shadow often appears as an actual double or twin or replicant, as in Poe's story "William Wilson" or Oscar Wilde's *The Picture of Dorian*

Gray. Such twin figures abound in literature, and also in film, and even in television series — as I recall, Data, the android in *Star Trek: The Next Generation,* was once supplied with a malevolent Shadow figure. All those "evil twin" plots, the Jungians would say, are about the Shadow.

WHICH OF COURSE has a bearing on stories about revenge, where Shadows run rampant. Who knows why Character A feels such an extreme loathing toward Character B? The Shadow knows, and until Character A knows too, and acknowledges the Shadow as a creature of his own making, he won't be free of it.

There's a whole genre of Elizabethan and Jacobean drama known as the Revenge Tragedy, and if you look at some of these plays you can see the principles of revenge in action. In general, the plots go in for overkill — quite literally — since one revenge leads to another, and the bodies pile up at an almost industrial rate. It's not just TIT FOR TAT, it's tit-for-tat for tit-for-tat for rat-a-tat-tat, as in the early crime stories of Dashiell Hammett. In previous chapters, I mentioned the trickle-down theory of wealth and the trickle-down theory of debt, but the Revenge Tragedy illustrates the trickle-down theory of revenge: relatively innocent bystanders get the stuff splashed all over them. *Hamlet* is among other things a Revenge Tragedy, but as usual Shakespeare takes something from elsewhere and redoes it in a surprising way: it's the slowness of the revenge, not its rapidity, that results in the dead-body pyramid at play's end.

Shakespeare also rewrites the Revenge Tragedy in *The Merchant of Venice* — a play so many-levelled and prickly that it's still inspiring heated controversy today. It's usual to say that every actor aspires to play Hamlet, but playing Shylock — who is either the hero or the villain of the piece, or possibly both, or neither — is arguably a greater challenge, for Shylock's complexities are many, and they've become more complex over time. How to play Shylock after the Nazis? Indeed, how to play Shylock, now that the interest-charging for which he's despised and reviled has become standard business practice?

The Merchant of Venice has all those props we've come to recognize as integral to debtor/creditor balances, both moral and financial — going way back to the weighing of the heart by the Ancient Egyptians and to the goddess Justice hoisting her scales outside the courts of law, and proceeding to the pledge left with the pawnbroker, and to the dubious written contract. The action of the play turns on the borrowing of a sum of money, and on the peculiar collateral demanded, and on the notion of fairness.

Shylock is a Jew and a moneylender. Two strokes against him for an Elizabethan author, or so you'd think. But Shakespeare is a very dodgy writer: ambiguity is his middle name. Did he realize that Shylock and Antonio are each other's Shadow figures? They are the only two characters who are left alone and uncoupled at the end of the play: everyone else marries someone. Are Antonio and Shylock married in a sense to each other? Unfortunately Shakespeare isn't around to give author interviews, so we'll never know.

The plot, insofar as it concerns a debt and the three main characters involved in this debt, is fairly simple. Antonio wishes to lend money to his friend Bassanio, but doesn't have ready cash, so he stands security for a loan from a third party: the moneylender Shylock, his long-time enemy. But instead of a money guarantee, Shylock requires a pound of Antonio's flesh, to be cut off next to his heart and weighed out in a scales if the loan isn't repaid by the due date. The merchant ships Antonio was counting on for cash flow go astray, the due date arrives, and Shylock demands his pound of flesh. Even when offered three times the money instead — as the price of "redeeming" Antonio, so he won't have to pay the forfeit of his life — Shylock still demands what's written in the contract. Money is not the point here. Only revenge will do.

Portia — the wife Bassanio has won with the aid of Shylock's money and his own wits — dresses up as a lawyer and pleads the case. First she urges mercy: the Jew must be merciful, she says. Shylock quite reasonably says, "Why must I?" Portia makes a lovely speech about mercy, which is however unconvincing, as such speeches usually are. Then she puts on her fine-print nitpicking lawyer boots: Shylock can have what's been agreed to, she says, but not a tittle more: he must weigh out the flesh, but he can't spill any blood, because it's not in the contract.

Shylock thus gets neither the pound of flesh nor the sum of the original debt. Not only that, as an "alien" designing against the life of a Venetian, his own life is forfeit by law. Portia and the judge let him off that one, as long as he turns Christian. But he has to give half of his wealth to the state — so often the beneficiary in such judgements — and will the other half of his worldly goods to his disobedient and thieving runaway daughter, Jessica, and the Christian man she's married.

Shylock isn't a Faust figure: he's made no pact with the Devil. There's a stock miser figure that goes all the way back to Roman New Comedy and persists through the medieval morality play as the character who portrays the sin of covetousness, and then turns up again as the Pantalone of Venetian *commedia dell'arte*, and thence to Molière's seventeenth-century play *The Miser*, but although Shylock shares a few of their outward characteristics, he isn't one of these. Previous miser figures are miserly because they're miserly, but Shylock is a Jew, and that changes much. From what I've said about the persecution of the Jews at the hands of rampaging mobs, it's clear that Shylock has legitimate reasons to worry about whether his house and his worldly goods and his daughter are locked up tight. If I'd been Shylock, I'd have been cautious about doling out the house keys too.

Antonio is usually interpreted as a good guy because he lends money without charging interest, but why give him points on that? As a Christian in the play's pretend "Venice" of that time, he wasn't *allowed* to charge interest!

He needn't have lent any money at all, of course. So by lending it he's undercutting Shylock's business, but not as a business rival. He isn't a business rival: he isn't in the *business* of moneylending at all, since he doesn't make anything by it. As far as I can see, he's doing it out of anti-Semitism. From the evidence in the play, he's been acting viciously toward Shylock for some time, both in word and in deed. He has projected onto Shylock — as his Shadow — the malice and the greediness that he himself possesses but can't acknowledge. He's made Shylock his whipping boy. That's why Shylock hates him — not just because he's been bringing down the rate of exchange.

Shakespeare does spell such things out for us. In *Othello*, for instance, the key to Iago's bad behaviour is in his name. Iago was the Spanish name for Saint James, who was known in Spain as Santiago the Moor-Killer. So Iago is a racist: that's why he does what he does. And Antonio does what he does in the moneylending way not only out of good fellowship toward the lendees but out of spite and vengefulness toward Shylock and all Jewish moneylenders, and all Jews.

Playing Antonio is as much of a challenge as playing Shylock: how to show Antonio as a nice guy but still keep in view the underlying motives for Shylock's vengeful actions as Shakespeare wrote them? Most productions downplay Antonio's anti-Semitism and that of his pals, but Richard Rose's version, presented at Stratford, Ontario, in 2007, gave this aspect its full due. Shylock was played by a Native North American, who didn't go in for the whining and grovelling and overacting that in the past made Shylock a semi-comic though despicable character, but instead presented a dignified, withdrawn Shylock who's been maimed and indeed driven somewhat crazy by the hatred of the society he's had to function in — much as many a Native North American has been. I thought this approach made total sense of the play. Most critics didn't like it, though: they so much wanted Antonio to be a regular fellow.

All three of the central characters violate the religions they purport to believe in. Antonio violates what is surely the central tenet of Christianity: love thy neighbour as thyself. Jesus pointedly told the story of the good Samaritan in this respect. Your neighbour wasn't just your co-religionist — *neighbour* was a category that included even those with whom you were at theological odds. Shylock is Antonio's neighbour, but Antonio does not treat him as such. As the old joke goes, "Christianity — great religion, just never been tried." Shylock is right when he says he's learned his vengefulness from the Christians that surround him: he has.

As for Shylock, he violates Mosaic law — the Deuteronomic law that says you shouldn't take a man's means of livelihood as pledge; that is, you can't — as part of a loan deal — imperil his life. It's a point Shylock himself makes at the end of the play, when he points out that Portia has deprived him of his power to make a living: "You take my life," he says. "When you do take the means whereby I live." This very same principle is incorporated in debt

and bankruptcy law today — you can't seize the tools necessary to a person's trade or business. Shylock is twice so
deprived: first, by the loss of his money — that is, his
working capital, which is his toolkit — and second, by the
stipulation that forces him to turn Christian, which cuts
him off from the ability to charge interest.

Portia would seem to be the best of the threesome.
She does make a lovely speech about mercy, which we
had to memorize in high school — the one beginning
"The quality of mercy is not strained." Nobody told me
"strained" meant "constrained," that is, forced, compelled,
or bound, so I came away with the image of a sieve, which
I've had some difficulty getting rid of ever since.

The counterpart to this speech of Portia's is Shylock's
famous speech:

> I am a Jew. Hath not a Jew eyes? Hath not a Jew hands,
> organs, dimensions, senses, affections, passions; fed
> with the same food, hurt with the same weapons, sub-
> ject to the same diseases, heal'd by the same means,
> warm'd and cool'd by the same winter and summer, as
> a Christian is? If you prick us, do we not bleed? If you
> tickle us, do we not laugh? If you poison us, do we not
> die? And if you wrong us, do we not revenge? If we are
> like you in the rest, we will resemble you in that.

When I studied this in school, I thought Shylock was
saying he was just as good as everyone else, which isn't
quite accurate. Instead he is saying he's just as human.

His body is the same as a human body, and his vengefulness, too, is the same as that of other people.

Portia's speech urges the claims of mercy over justice,
and it sounds very sweet; but what it's saying is, in effect,
that Shylock has to be more merciful than everyone else
has been to him. When Shylock can't manage this, Portia
undercuts her elevation of the quality of mercy by reverting to eye-for-an-eye tit-for-tattery justice, and more.
True, some mercy does come out of the affair: Antonio is
the one who seems to have had his vindictiveness blunted
by his near-death experience, and Shylock remains alive;
though how he will manage to make a living in future is
an interesting question.

He must, however, be absolved of the charge of covetousness. He's offered three times the sum of the debt to
buy off the pound of flesh, and he refuses. He thus violates
the code of business practice — make a profit, whatever
else — as well as the Mosaic code of the redemption of
pawned objects, and opts for vengeance instead. As James
Buchan comments, in his astute analysis of *The Merchant
of Venice* in *Frozen Desire*, his fascinating book about the
nature of money, "At precisely that moment when he must
succeed, Shylock falls prey to that violence that money
was invented to replace. I cannot stress the point too fully.
The pound of flesh is not a collateral security...for it cannot be sequestered and turned into money. Instead it is
an insane and primitive forfeit...in which money does
not compensate an insult to the body but the other way
around: not blood-money but money-blood."

THERE ARE TWO antidotes to the endless chain reaction of revenge and counter-revenge. One is through the courts of law, which are supposed to settle questions of the weighing and measuring and resolving of debtor/creditor issues in a fair and equitable way. Whether they always do so is of course open to a lot of questions, but in theory that is their function.

The other antidote is more radical. It is told of Nelson Mandela that, after much persecution, and when he was finally freed from the prison where he'd been put by the apartheid government in South Africa, he said to himself that he had to forgive all those who had wronged him by the time he reached the prison gates or he would never be free of them. Why? Because he'd be bound to them by the chains of vengeance. They and he would still be twin Shadow figures, joined at the hip. In other words, the antidote to revenge is not justice but forgiveness. How many times must you forgive? someone asked Jesus of Nazareth. Seventy times seven, or as many times as it takes, was the answer. So Portia was right in principle, although she herself could not follow through.

Muslim religious law allows the family members of a murdered person to participate in the sentencing of the murderer: they can choose clemency if they wish, and it is recognized that this choice is a noble one, and will free them from their anger and sense of victimization. There are many other cultural examples in which a life is not taken in exchange for a life. A Native North American group presented a Proclamation of Forgiveness to the United States as recently as 2005, for instance — if they listed all the things to be forgiven I expect it was rather long — and I need hardly mention the astonishing Truth and Reconciliation process that has gone on in South Africa since the end of apartheid. You may think that all of this forgiveness stuff is watery-eyed idealism of the clap-if-you-believe-in-fairies variety, but if the forgiveness is sincerely given and sincerely received — both parts are admittedly difficult — it does appear to have a liberating effect. As we've noted, the desire for revenge is a heavy chain, and revenge itself leads to a chain reaction. Forgiveness cuts the chain.

Now take a deep breath, close your eyes, and try the following exercise in historical revisionism. It's the eleventh of September 2001. After two planes have flown into them, the Twin Towers have collapsed in billows of smoke and fire. Vengeful messages have been disseminated by al-Qaeda. The president of the United States goes on international television and says,

> We have suffered a grievous loss — a blow has been struck at us that was motivated by a obsessive desire to harm us. We realize that this was the work of a small group of fanatics. Other nations might bomb the stuffing out of the civilian population where those fanatics are at present located, but we recognize the futility of such an action. Nor will we accuse any bystander nation of having been involved. We realize that acts of

vengeance recoil upon the heads of the inventors, and we do not wish to perpetuate a chain reaction of revenge. Therefore we will forgive.

Just imagine the impact of taking such a position, not that there was a snowball's chance in Hell of this ever happening. Now imagine how much different the world would have been today if that position had in fact been taken. No ongoing Iraq war. No impasse in Afghanistan. And above all, no ballooning and ruinous and nation-weakening and out-of-control big fat American debt.

Where will it all end? you are doubtless asking yourself. That depends on what you mean by "all." As for this book, it will end with the next and last chapter, which will attempt to examine what happens when the debit and credit balances get even further out of control. This last chapter is called "Payback." I looked this word up on the Web and, in addition to several movies of that name, I found a site called ThePayback.com, which bills itself as "your home for all of your revenge needs." You can order anything over the Internet now, it seems, including "dead fish," "prank packages," and "rude lottery tickets."

But my final chapter will not be about sending a box of wilted roses to your detested ex-lover. It's more on the order of the mills of the gods, which grind very slowly, though they grind exceeding small.

(FIVE)

PAYBACK

THE OVERALL SUBJECT of this book is what I've been thinking of as the debtor/creditor twinship, considered in its
broadest aspect; and, as a prelude to this final chapter, I'd
like to recap some of the key themes touched on so far.

The first chapter, "Ancient Balances," dealt with our
human sense of fairness, balance, and justice, a sense that
is very old. Its origins may well be prehuman — a view
that scientific studies of monkey and chimpanzee behaviour would tend to support. These animals have strong
opinions about the distribution of goods and the fair rate
of exchange — refusing to trade a cucumber slice for a
pebble, for instance, when the neighbour is getting a grape,
and remembering who owes them favours in return for
favours granted. I postulated that none of our many systems of debt and credit could exist without an innate
human module that evaluates fairness and unfairness and
strives for balance: otherwise nobody would either lend or
pay back. Among solitary animals such as porcupines, a

brain module like this would serve no purpose, but among social animals such as ourselves, dependent as we are on give and take, it does seem necessary. Also necessary is a sense of payback—what negative action you will take in case of a failure to return what is owed.

On such early foundations, many elaborate systems of debts and repayments have been constructed; for instance, the post-mortem judging of the soul among the Ancient Egyptians, in which the heart was weighed against the goddess of truth, justice, balance, right behaviour, and the order of the cosmos, and, if found wanting, was eaten by a monster crocodile god.

So some debts are not money debts: they are moral debts, or debts having to do with imbalances in the right order of things. Thus, in any consideration of debt, the concept of the balance is pivotal: debtor and creditor are two sides of a single entity, one cannot exist without the other, and exchanges between them—in a healthy economy or society or ecosystem—tend toward equilibrium.

The second chapter, "Debt and Sin," explored, as you might expect, the connection between debt and sin. Which is morally worse, to be a debtor or to be a creditor? Sinfulness has been attributed to both. This chapter also examined the connection between debt and memory, and thus between debt and written contracts—leading naturally to a long-standing theme in Western culture, the pact with the Devil, which I proposed as the first buy-now, pay-later scheme—a prime example being that of Doctor Faustus. A Faustian bargain is one in which you exchange your soul or something equally vital for a lot of glitzy but ultimately worthless short-term junk. I also explored the notion of redemption — a concept that applies to pawnshop practices as well as to redeemed slaves and redeemed souls.

In the third chapter, "Debt as Plot," I considered the Faustian bargain in more detail — particularly through the stories of Christopher Marlowe's Doctor Faustus and Charles Dickens's Ebenezer Scrooge, the latter being, I proposed, a reverse image of the former. Debt was traced as a governing leitmotif of Western fiction, especially that of the nineteenth century — a century in which, capitalism having triumphed and money having become the measure of most things, debt played a significant role in the lives of actual people. In the nineteenth century, industrial mills increased and multiplied, and drove the capitalist expansion, so I also discussed the sinister attributes traditionally attached to millers — who were thought of as cheats and probably as Devil's-pact-makers, since they seemed to be able to spin money out of nothing. Mills and millers were linked to the magical mills of folklore, that spew out anything you order up but are very difficult to stop. I concluded this chapter with a reference to the mills of the gods — those mills that grind slowly but very thoroughly. Most people interpret this ancient Greek saying to mean that the retribution for bad behaviour may be a long time coming, but when it does arrive it will be devastating.

This energizing thought led to the fourth chapter, "The Shadow Side," in which I touched upon the nastier forms of debt and credit account balancing. These included debtors' prisons, criminal loan-shark collection tactics, liquidating your creditors, rebelling against your rulers when the taxes they imposed were too heavy or too unfair, and — stepping outside the financial border altogether into an area in which money payment simply doesn't apply — vindictive, blood-soaked revenge.

And now we come to "Payback," my fifth and final chapter. I'll try to make this as painless as possible. No, on second thought, I won't do that: because if it were painless, it wouldn't be about payback, would it?

IN MY PART of the world we have a ritual interchange that goes like this:

First person: "Lovely weather we're having."

Second person: "We'll pay for it later."

My part of the world being Canada, where there is a great deal of weather, we always do pay for it later. One person has commented, "That's not Canadian, it's just Presbyterian." Nevertheless, it's a widespread saying among us.

What this ritual interchange reveals is a larger habit of thinking about the more enjoyable things in life: they're only on loan or acquired on credit, and sooner or later the date when they must be paid for will roll around. And that is what this chapter is about. It's about pay-up time. Or payback time, supposing that you haven't paid up. In any case, the time when whatever is on one side of the balance is weighed against whatever is on the other side — whether it's your heart, your soul, or your debts — and the final reckoning is made.

EVERY DEBT COMES with a date on which payment is due. Otherwise the creditor would never be able to collect, and would therefore never lend anything, and the whole system of borrowing and repaying would stop cold. In the financial services industries, the due date is written right on the mortgage or the loan papers or the credit card agreement. You must pay by that date, or you'll have to renew the loan; or, if you go overtime on your credit card charges, the interest shoots up, and then things can quickly get unpleasant.

Other sorts of debt also have due dates. In fact, debts of every kind are always coupled with the symbolisms of time and counting and numbers. In the Biblical Book of Daniel, a disembodied hand appears at Belshazzar's feast, and it writes on the wall: *Numbered, numbered, weighed, divided.* The prophet Daniel interprets this to mean that Belshazzar's kingdom has been numbered, and is finished — in other words, his number is up — and he's been weighed in the balance — the same kind of soul or heart or sin balance that the Ancient Egyptians used, we suppose — and the next day, payback arrives: Belshazzar is killed, and his kingdom is divided.

Calendars, clocks, bells ringing the hour: these mark time, and time runs out, for mortal life as well as for debts. That grandfather clock that was too large for the shelf so it stood ninety years on the floor was brought from the shop on the day that the grandfather was born, and went *tick tock, tick tock*, ninety years without slumbering, *tick tock, tick tock*, his life seconds numbering, just like a heartbeat; but it stopped short, never to go again, when the old man died. (I learned some memorable songs in grade three.)

The medieval figure of Death carries an hourglass as well as a scythe, and the hourglass signifies that the sands of time — your time — are finite and are running fast. Time's winged chariot is constantly hurrying near. In Edgar Allan Poe's story "The Masque of the Red Death," in which Prince Prospero and his thousand hand-picked revellers hoping to flee the plague move from one brightly coloured room of the Prince's palace to another, there's an enormous ebony clock in the seventh and final room. (Why seven? The seven ages of man would be my guess.) This foreboding clock also goes *tick tock*, and then it goes *bong* twelve times, because it's midnight — that mystic hour — and then everyone in the place sprouts red spots and keels over, because you can run but you can't hide. Not from Time and his or her Siamese-twin brother or sister, Death. (Poe's clock, like the ninety-year-old grand-father's, and the watches and clocks in so many murder mysteries — the ones with the bullet holes in them — stops with the last heartbeat.)

So never ask for whom the bell tolls, as the seventeenth-century poet John Donne said. It tolls for thee. Or it will. And then it will stop tolling, just like all those literary clocks.

Time is a condition of the life of our physical bodies: without it we can't live — we'd be frozen, like statues, because we wouldn't be able to change; but at the end of time — our time — we don't need Time any more. There are no clocks in Heaven. Nor are there any in Hell. In both, everything is always Now. Or so goes the rumour. In Heaven, there are no debts — all have been paid, one way or another — but in Hell there's nothing but debts, and a great deal of payment is exacted, though you can't ever get all paid up. You have to pay, and pay, and keep on paying. So Hell is like an infernal maxed-out credit card that multiplies the charges endlessly.

Here is Marlowe's Doctor Faustus, speaking on the due date of his loan contract with Mephistopheles. He's pondering the relentlessness of time, though he's also longing eloquently for an extension of it:

> I writ them a bill with mine own blood: the date
> is expired; the time will come, and he will fetch me....
> Ah, Faustus,
> Now hast thou but one bare hour to live,
> And then thou must be damn'd perpetually!
> Stand still, you ever-moving spheres of heaven,
> That time may cease, and midnight never come;
> Fair Nature's eye, rise, rise again, and make

Perpetual day; or let this hour be but
A year, a month, a week, a natural day,
That Faustus may repent and save his soul!
O lente, lente currite, noctis equi!
The stars move still, time runs, the clock will strike,
The devil will come, and Faustus must be damn'd.

The Latin line in this speech is a snippet of sad and yearning irony, coming as it does from a poem of Ovid's in which he's asking the horses of the night — those that draw Time's winged chariot — to run slowly. This way the night will stretch out very long, and he'll be able to spend more time in bed with his mistress. But the invocation doesn't work for poor Doctor Faustus: time marches relentlessly on, time flies, and not only the clock but the midnight bell strikes, and the dreaded payment falls due.

As I've said earlier, there's good reason to believe that Marlowe's Doctor Faustus and Dickens's Ebenezer Scrooge are mirror images of each other — everything Faustus does, Scrooge does backwards. And so it is with Time. What Faustus longs for — that Time will become rubbery and stretch out, so that the due date on his contract won't arrive and he won't have to pay over his body and soul to Mephistopheles — this rubberiness of time is something Scrooge actually gets.

The fateful hour for both men is between twelve midnight and one. Among those who follow the more winding paths of mythological association, twelve midnight signals the beginning of what is known as a hinge moment. This phrase now means a turning point, but I am using it in an older sense, dating from a period when time was thought to open and close at certain moments — Halloween and the solstices, for instance — when the actual doors between our world and other worlds swung open on their hinges; and that's the hour during which Faust is torn apart by demons.

It's this same hour that's so important for Ebenezer Scrooge, who receives his first two Spirits of Christmas at what he thinks is one o'clock in the morning on two successive nights — the first being Christmas Eve — and the third at twelve midnight on the third night; but when he wakes, the three nights have been folded into one, and what should have been two days after Christmas is still only Christmas morning. Time for Scrooge has run more slowly, so that he's accomplished in one night what should have taken three; and in the course of that one night he has lived over his whole life, and caught a glimpse of his potential future death, and then he's been snapped back into the present. Thus his payment date has been postponed, and he finds himself entering anew into the world — a world he can finally embrace as his own.

"Yes! and the bedpost was his own," he thinks. "The bed was his own, the room was his own. Best and happiest of all, the Time before him was his own, to make amends in." He then announces that he doesn't know what day of the month it is, and he's as merry as a schoolboy, and in addition to that, he's a baby. At which point there's a confusion of bell-ringing; but these are not the solemn tolling bells that announce a death, nor are they marking the relentless passing of Time. Instead they are bells of celebration. They're celebrating a birth — two births, in fact: that of Jesus, and that of the reborn baby Scrooge. They're also celebrating the suspension of the ordinary rules of time and thus the ordinary rules of debt. Scrooge has had a reprieve. He's been given extra time — an extra life, in fact. And now he will use it to pay back what he's taken; to make, as he says "amends."

Let's pause here to ponder the derivation of the word "amends." According to the *Oxford English Dictionary*, "amends" comes from a word that originally meant a payment, in money or goods, for something you'd done wrong. By making amends then, Scrooge is paying a moral debt. To whom does he owe this debt, and why? In Dickens's view, he owes it to his fellow man: he's been on the take from other people all his life — that's where his fortune has come from — but he's never given anything back. By being a creditor of such magnitude in the financial sense, he himself has become a debtor in the moral sense, and it's this realization that's at the core of his transformation. Money isn't the only thing that must flow and circulate in order to have value: good turns and gifts must also flow and circulate — just as they do among chimpanzees — for any social system to remain in balance.

We know what Scrooge uses his extra time for — turkey purchasing, Tiny Tim saving, charity subscription giving, party game participation, and Bob Cratchit salary

raising; in short, fellow feeling for his fellow man, signalled in some cases by the amounts he's prepared to
dispense. We readers and viewers are always pleased
when we reach this part of the story: it gives us a warm,
comfy, rum-punch kind of feeling, and sentimental tears
are shed, by me at any rate. But then the twinkling snow-
lit scene recedes, and we close the book or leave the theatre
or turn off the TV and don't think much more about it,
because the story of Scrooge is after all an outdated children's tale, and we must get back to grown-up real life.

But let's stay with Scrooge for a moment, and try a
small mental exercise. Some people are in the habit of
saying, "What would Jesus do?" Which sounds admirably
pious, though sometimes the questioners get curious
answers — bomb Iran, screw the poor, burn a church, tell
smear-tactic lies about your political opponents, try a little torture, and so forth. It's kind of hard to imagine Jesus
standing over a tied-up prisoner of war and zapping him
or her with a cattle prod. Call me an old-fashioned stick-
ler, but in the official texts about him, Jesus is on the
receiving end of such tactics, not on the doling-out end.

Most of us are not very much like Jesus, so it's difficult for us to imagine what Jesus actually would do if he
were present in the flesh. But though we're not very
much like Jesus, we are in fact quite a lot like Scrooge. So
what would Scrooge do if he were here with us today,
and if he faced the problems we ourselves are now facing,
not to mention the payback date that's moving so rapidly in our direction? And if he'd been given extra time

to make amends, what form might those amends take? Would Scrooge feel he needed to pay a moral debt to his fellow men, or would he come to realize that there were other kinds of debts to be paid by him as well?

Let's find out.

AS YOU KNOW, there are two Scrooges. There's the squeezing, wrenching, grasping, scraping, clutching, covetous old sinner we meet first in the story about him — I'll call this one "Scrooge Original," following the lead of certain soft-drink and potato-chip companies. Then there's the second Scrooge, the one that emerges after his born-again experience. I'll call him "Scrooge Lite," because in the Arthur Rackham illustrations, Scrooge Original is shown crouched over a heavy bag of money, but Scrooge Lite is shown standing erect with both hands open — he's become open-handed — and he's happy and smiling, lighter both in purse and in spirit. Modern research backs up Dickens and Rackham — apparently rich people are not made happier simply by having a lot of wealth, but they *are* made happier when they give some of their wealth away. I read about this phenomenon in a newspaper, so it must be true.

If you yourself want to become really happy by using this method, I suggest that you help save the albatross from extinction. It can be done.

It can be done today, that is. Tomorrow it may not be possible, because saving a species from extinction also has a date stamp on it, just like debt and mortal life.

Anyway, those are the two traditional Scrooges: Scrooge Original, Scrooge Lite. But let's contemplate a third Scrooge: Scrooge as he would be if he were among us in the early twenty-first century. I'll call this one "Scrooge Nouveau," because when you're introducing a high-end quality product it's just as well to make it sound a little French.

Scrooge Nouveau is the same age as Scrooge Original, but he doesn't look it. He looks much younger, because, unlike Scrooge Original, he does spend his money: he spends it on himself. So he's had a hair transplant, and some facial adjustment, and his skin is tanned from the many voyages he's taken on his private yacht, and his very white and expertly restored teeth gleam eerily in the dark.

I was going to give him a golf course all of his very own, but that wouldn't work, because a golf course with only one player on it isn't really a golf course, just as an anthill with only one ant isn't really an anthill; and Scrooge Nouveau wouldn't want to play with anyone else, since he doesn't take to the idea of losing, even in theory. Sometimes he goes hunting and shoots animals, but only from a safe distance. In his recreational tastes he's much like Machiavelli's Renaissance prince, though he doesn't poison people. Or not directly. He only poisons them as a regrettable but inevitable side effect of cost-benefit analysis: it would cost too much not to poison them, and the subsequent lawsuits can be written off as a business expense.

Unlike Scrooge Original, Scrooge Nouveau isn't cantankerous, or not on the surface. There's a book out now that tells you how to get very, very rich by acting like an A — dollar sign, dollar sign — H-O-L-E, but Scrooge Nouveau is already very rich, so he doesn't have to act like an A — dollar sign, dollar sign — H-O-L-E. He did have to act like one earlier — that's how he got very, very rich — but now he has people who do that for him. So he's not gruff and surly, and he isn't rude to charity seekers, the way Scrooge Original was. If he doesn't want to see such people, he's simply in a meeting.

If today's corporate laws had existed in 1843, Scrooge Original would have had a corporation instead of a firm — so much more protective for him! — but the limited-liability corporation didn't appear until 1854 and didn't achieve its full complement of legal tools until the late nineteenth century. So Scrooge Original was a partner in a firm — Scrooge and Marley, it was called. From the order of the names we assume that Scrooge was the senior partner and would have had the corner office if he'd gone in for such things. But he didn't: Scrooge Original's office was as dismal and dingy and stingy as everything else about him.

But Scrooge Nouveau lives in the twenty-first century, so he does have a corner office, and he doesn't have a firm. He has a corporation. In fact, he has many of them. He collects them — it's a hobby of his. He doesn't much care what they make, so long as they make money.

Some of Scrooge Nouveau's wealth has gone to the four ex-Mrs. Scrooges that feature so prominently in celebrity magazines about the lifestyles of the rich and famous. Two of these ex-wives have given bitchy tell-all interviews about Scrooge, who likes this kind of attention, in moderation, because he likes anything about himself. But it's not his fault that he's a self-centred narcissist: he grew up surrounded by advertisements that told him he was worth it, and that he owed it to himself. He's on his fifth Mrs. Scrooge now. She's twenty-two, a stunning girl with very long legs. He owes it to himself, because he's worth it.

These common twenty-first-century locutions come, of course, directly from the language of valuation — worth it to whom, and how much? — and also from the language of debt. Scrooge owes it to himself — he's his own debtor and creditor rolled into one. What has he borrowed from himself? Time and effort, we suppose — the same time and effort that have allowed him to increase the fortune he inherited from Scrooge Original through Scrooge's nephew, Fred. So now he can pay himself back by giving himself this mysterious "it" — usually whatever's in the ad. He owes "it" to himself, but, by extension, he doesn't owe a plugged nickel to anyone else. That is his view.

We join Scrooge Nouveau in his lavish villa, some-where in — where? — let's say Tuscany, though he's thinking of selling this joint because the neighbourhood's getting cluttered up with tycoons of lesser worth than himself whose show-off globs of architecture are ruining the vistas. Mrs. Scrooge the Fifth is in Milan, shopping for state-of-the-art stiletto heels. Scrooge Nouveau has spent the afternoon with one of his CEOs, whose name is Bob Cratchit — an overpaid and useful but envious and cringing little suck, in Scrooge Nouveau's opinion. Cratchit has a brash, badly dressed wife and a mob of obnoxious children, the youngest of whom, Timmy, is a prodigious whiner. Scrooge regularly ignores Bob's hints that this horde of snivelling Cratchit moppets be invited to swim in his pool.

It's evening. Scrooge has enjoyed a modest dinner of Chilean sea bass — an almost extinct fish, but delicious, and anyway somebody's got to eat it, because it's already dead, so why waste it? He's relaxing over a mellow but fruity and audaciously nosed postprandial glass of (fill in the vintage yourself), when he hears a foreboding sound and smells a horrible smell. The sound is a wet, slurping, sucking sound, as of someone trudging through a swamp; the smell is the smell of decay. And the whole sideshow is coming up the marble staircase of the villa, straight toward him.

What was in that bottle of (fill in the vintage yourself) anyway? thinks Scrooge. He casts his mind back to his youthful days of drug experimentation. He barely has time to process his inner defence — "I never inhaled!"— when his former corporate partner, Jake Marley — dead these many years, having had a heart attack on the treadmill in the hi-tech corporate gym — materializes in the armchair facing his. Wound around him and trailing on the floor is a long chain made of stinking fish, wildlife specimens that are falling apart, and the skulls and hair of developing-world peasants.

"Jake!" says Scrooge Nouveau. "You're dripping on my priceless oriental carpet! What are you doing here anyway, and why are you wearing that trash heap?"

"I wear the trash heap I forged in life," says Marley. "You ought to see yours! It's three times as long and stinky as mine. And I've come to warn you, in order that you may escape my fate. Three Spirits will visit you."

"Do they have appointments?" says Scrooge Nouveau, vowing that if they do he'll fire his executive assistant. "I can't see them. I'll be in a meeting."

"Expect the first Spirit tonight when the clock strikes one," says Jake Marley, vanishing in a puff of stench. Scrooge looks out the window, sees a lot of decomposing codfish flying through the air with a chair of the board attached to each one, takes a shower in his marble bathroom to clear his head, pops a sleeping pill, and conks out in his authentic and costly seventeenth-century four-poster bed.

None of this keeps the first Spirit from appearing at his bedside at 1 a.m. sharp. She's female — a pleasant-looking damsel, clad in green, with a wreath of flowers in her hair. She looks like an all-natural-and-organic-shampoo ad. Maybe this won't be so bad, thinks Scrooge. "Care to join me?" he says to her, indicating his bed. He owes this to himself. The fifth Mrs. Scrooge need never find out, and if she does, so what — he can afford her displeasure.

"I am the Spirit of Earth Day Past," says the Spirit. "Rise, and walk with me."

Scrooge is about to protest that he needs to put on his thousand-dollar customized running shoes if he's going to do anything as challenging as walking, when he finds himself yanked out the window and flying through the air.

"There wasn't any effing Earth Day in the past!" he barks at the Spirit, now that he's had time to think about it.

"Such a day was not needed," says the Spirit as they glide above the clouds. "Imagine taking only one day in which to honour the Earth! It's like Mother's Day — dump a card and some flowers on the old hen once a year, then exploit her the rest of the time. But in ancient societies, the debt we owe to the Earth was remembered at all seasons. Each religion paid tribute to the sacredness of the Earth, and acknowledged with gratitude that everything people ate, drank, and breathed came from it through providence. Unless people treated the gifts given by the natural world with respect, and refrained from wastefulness and greed, divine displeasure would follow, signalled by drought, disease, and famine. In addition to that, earlier peoples felt they had to pay back what they'd received. This is where the idea of sacrifice came from: human sacrifice, in certain South American tribal cultures, is still referred to as 'feeding the earth.' The prevailing ethos was that there was a debt, and it had to be repaid, and repaid regularly, or the benefits that were given would be withheld."

Scrooge is annoyed with himself: he shouldn't have raised the subject and let himself in for such a big chunk of self-righteous preaching. "Where are we?" he says. They seem to be caught in a flickering maze of light and darkness.

"We're moving through Time," says the Spirit. "Backward. Close your eyes if it makes you dizzy."

"Well, anyway," says Scrooge. "Civilization advanced. We grew out of that crude sacrifice stuff. We approach things rationally now, what with science, and cost-benefit analysis, and the use of debt as a sophisticated investment vehicle, and..."

The Spirit smiles. "Nature is an expert in cost-benefit analysis," she says. "Although she does her accounting a little differently. As for debts, she always collects in the long run. The rationality you cite dates back a mere two centuries, when people began substituting something called 'the Market' for God, attributing the same characteristics to it: all-knowingness, always-rightness, and the ability to make something called 'corrections,' which, like the divine punishments of old, had the effect of wiping out a great many people. Enlightened people came to believe that the Earth was nothing more than an assemblage of machines, and therefore that everything in it, animal life included, existed only to be re-engineered to do Man's will and work—like a water mill. Even in the early twentieth century, the scientists were telling us — for example — that animals had no emotions, and could thus be treated as if they were inanimate objects. Which was much like what used to be said of the lower classes in England, and of slaves everywhere.

"However, the sense of a living Earth persisted into fairly modern times, if only via the language. When a person died, it was said, 'He has paid his debt to Nature.' In other words, the physical body had merely been borrowed — never owned outright — and death was the means whereby the loan was paid back. Which is literally true, as long as the relatives don't cremate the corpse, or seal it into an airtight burial vault. But if it's allowed to dissolve, and return to the elements..."

Scrooge feels a little sick. He's never pictured his own body as being borrowed, and he certainly doesn't like to think of it as having to be paid back in such a distressing way. It's his to hold in perpetuity, and to improve, like a piece of real estate. He's made quite a big investment in it! He understands there are some bioengineers working on the Immortality Project right now, and as soon as they've got real results, he'll buy in. Why shouldn't his body keep on working for him forever? "Can we talk about something else?" he says.

"Certainly," says the Spirit. "Our first stop is Athens. It's the sixth century B.C.E."

Scrooge finds himself in a plain but clean room, open to the sea and sky beyond. Some old geezer in a bedsheet is pondering.

"This man is Solon," says the Spirit, "the saviour of Athens. The aristocracy have controlled the government for a long time, and have made laws that benefit themselves. This has allowed them to corner a disproportionate amount of the state's wealth. During years of bad harvests, they've driven the poorer farmers deeper and deeper into debt, and then into serfdom and slavery. The result has been economic stagnation."

"I thought you were an Earth Day spirit," says Scrooge. "Why are you lecturing me on economics?"

"As Charles Darwin said, 'The economy shown by Nature in her resources is striking,'" says the Spirit. "All wealth comes from Nature. Without it, there wouldn't be any economics. The primary wealth is food, not money. Therefore anything that concerns the handling of the land also concerns me."

This is a novel way of thinking, for Scrooge. He's always assumed that food came from restaurants, or else from upmarket delicatessen grocers.

"Solon was long held to be the greatest lawmaker of the Athenians," says the Spirit. "Right now, he's thinking about how to solve the nation's problems by cancelling the massive debt structure that has enriched some, but impoverished everyone else. And that's what he finally did. In essence, he wiped the debt-slate clean."

"You mean, he defaulted?" says Scrooge. He shudders, envisioning what would happen to his own investment portfolio under these circumstances.

"Absolutely," says the Spirit. "The alternative would have been a blood-soaked and costly revolution, because the Athenian peasants had been ground down too far. When debt becomes too highly concentrated in the hands of a few, the accounts must be balanced peacefully, or chaos and destruction will be the result. In this case, the rich and powerful who'd taken so much over so many years were forced to pay back by having their claims destroyed, and the result was renewed prosperity for the community. That's one form of account balancing. Now let me show you another."

Time flickers again, and they're looking down at a medieval port city.

"Caffa," says the Spirit, "on the coast of the Black Sea — a colony founded by the Genoese to exploit the overland trade from the Far East. The year is 1347. A great many people down there are already paying their debts to Nature."

Scrooge and the Spirit swoop low over Caffa. The city is in turmoil: it has barely survived a Mongol siege, but not before being infected with the Black Death from the virus-ridden besiegers. Now people are dropping like flies in the narrow, overcrowded, filthy streets, while, in the harbour, crowds of panic-stricken citizens are pushing their way onto the ships, hoping they can escape.

"Why have you brought me here?" says Scrooge. "When can we leave?" The stench arising from Caffa is ten times as awful as the stench of Jake Marley's Ghost.

"The Black Death is about to invade Europe," says the Spirit of Earth Day Past. "No country will be spared. The plague will come by sea—these Genoese galleys from Caffa will spread it—and then it will run like wildfire over the whole continent. The cities there are overcrowded and unsanitary, and the countries are overpopulated and malnourished, having exhausted the food resources available to them. Also, the immune systems of many of those now living were weakened in their childhoods, during the Great Famine of 1315–16, when torrential rains ruined the harvests and hundreds of thousands died. Pandemic plagues love overcrowding, ecological disasters, and victims weakened by malnutrition. In two years, by the time the first wave of the Great Mortality is over, half of the people now living will be dead. Cities will be emptied. A great many animals and birds will also die. Farms will fall into ruin; forests will grow over them. The entire landscape of Europe will be transformed."

This thing is turning into a television documentary of the kind Scrooge always switches off—poor people, famines, diseases and disasters, all of that—because why dwell on such negative details? He would really, really like to be back in his own bed, or one of his beds. But instead they're fast-forwarding through the Black Death, which is very gruesome. Some people are coughing blood, others are turning black, still others are sprouting huge boils.

"When any bad situation is getting worse," says the Spirit—a sententious girl, as such Spirits tend to be—

"It *wasn't* all bad," says the Spirit, reading his thoughts. "Death pays all debts, and cancels a lot of them, so a great deal of working capital was eventually freed up. For the survivors, wages rose, due to a shortage of labour, and the cumbersome and demeaning feudal system came to an end. The position of women improved — jobs were opened to them, as they were during the First and Second World Wars. A period of technical innovation was inaugurated, for good or ill. And just think of the artistic masterpieces inspired by the Great Mortality: Boccaccio's *Decameron Nights*, Albert Camus's novel *The Plague*, the Swedish film director Ingmar Bergman's masterpiece *The Seventh Seal*. . . . It's an ill plague that blows no good."

"I'd rather skip the masterpieces and do without the plague," says Scrooge.

"Maybe a pandemic plague is part of Nature's cost-benefit analysis," says the Spirit. "A way of wiping the slate clean and balancing the accounts. When Mankind becomes too irritating — too numerous, too filthy, too destructive to the Earth — a plague results. Farm animals crowded together are equally prone to disease. Think of a cat coughing up a hairball and you get the picture."

This cat's-hairball metaphor is not flattering to humanity, of which Scrooge suddenly feels a part for the first time in his life. But now the Spirit has hauled him up into the clouds again, and they've left the plague-ridden cities of the fourteenth century behind them.

THE SPIRIT OF Earth Day Past takes Scrooge on a rapid journey through time and space. First they visit North America in 1793 to watch an episode in the destruction of the passenger pigeon — enormous flocks of birds are shot down and left to lie, many more than can ever be gathered up and eaten. "The Lord won't see the waste of His creatures for nothing, and right will be done to the pigeons, as well as others, by and by," says a tall, rustic-looking old man who's standing by. "I call it sinful and wasty, to catch more than can be eat."

"Leatherstocking," says the Spirit, "from *The Pioneers*, an 1832 novel by James Fenimore Cooper."

"But he's just a character in a book!" says Scrooge.

"So are you," says the Spirit reprovingly. She's got a point, thinks Scrooge. "I wished to show you that even in abundant North America — abundant at that time — people were already thinking about the right and wrong uses of what is now called 'natural capital.'"

Next they witness the arrival in Europe of the cheap and nutritious potato from the New World. It spreads rapidly, fuelling a population explosion that more than refills the countries and cities, despite new waves of plague and other high-mortality diseases — tuberculosis, diphtheria, smallpox, typhoid, cholera, syphilis, and more. Scrooge decides that the Spirit of Earth Day Past is a sicko. He has to watch as the 1840s potato blight arrives, ravaging Ireland and signalling — says the Spirit — the hazards of monocropping, which Nature has always disliked. It's folly,

says the Spirit, to become dependent on just a few crops —
wheat, rice, corn, and soy, for instance, as in the twenty-first
century — because a blight can cause instant famines.

Leaving the howling and dying Irish behind, Scrooge
and the Spirit fly over London, where, as in time-lapse
photography, Scrooge witnesses the rise of the factories
with their smoking chimneys, and the subsequent overcrowding, and the misery caused by the boom-and-bust
cycling of early capitalism. Deformed, greenish children
teem in smog-choked slums; families sleep fifteen to an
airless, fetid room. Sewage runs in the open gutters.

"How can people live like that?" says Scrooge. This is
repulsive.

"What choice did they have?" says the Spirit. "There
was no social safety net."

"Well, private philanthropy could step in..." says
Scrooge, who's a great believer in removing the respon-
sibility for social inequities — not to mention tax
burdens — from people such as himself.

"'Pity would be no more, / If we did not make somebody Poor; / And Mercy no more could be / If all were as
happy as we,'" murmurs the Spirit.

"What?" says Scrooge.

"A little light verse," says the Spirit. "William Blake.
Now my travels with you are almost over. I can show you
only one more scene. The year is 1972. The place is Toronto,
Canada."

Time flickers, and Scrooge finds himself in a modern-
looking room. No more withered-up children, no plague

victims, no rotting potatoes, which is a relief. Only a sixty-three-year-old woman reading a newspaper. She cuts out an article, which she folds and tucks into an envelope. She seals the envelope, writes the date on it, then goes downstairs to her cellar and puts it into a steamer trunk.

"What did it say?" asks Scrooge. "That thing she cut out of the paper?"

BUT THE CLOCK strikes one, again, and the Spirit of Earth Day Past wavers and dissolves, and then re-forms — except that now she's a man. Scrooge hates these sex-change things: they give him the willies.

"Yo, Scrooge baby," says the man, West Coastishly. "I am the Spirit of Earth Day Present. Just call me the S of EDP." He's wearing a bicycle helmet and a hemp T-shirt that says *Hug My Tree*. In one hand he's carrying a use-again shopping bag made from recycled plastic pop bottles, and in the other he holds a coffee cup that says *Songbird-friendly Shade-grown Fair-trade Pesticide-free Organic*. He looks a little like David Suzuki, and a little like Al Gore, and also a little like Prince Charles, in his organic farmer guise. "So," he continues, "which piece of disaster-in-the-making do you want to visit first?"

Scrooge wishes to say "None of them," but he realizes by now that this is not an option. "You choose," he says gruffly. This guy seems mild enough, but there's something deeply weird about him — like a hippie who's gone through a teleportation device and come out with a few parts scrambled.

"Okay," says the Spirit, and the next moment Scrooge finds himself at the bottom of the ocean. A huge net is being dragged across the sea floor, destroying everything in its path. Ahead of it bloom undersea forests and their hundreds and thousands of living creatures, both plant and animal; behind it is a desert. The net is pulled to the surface and most of the dead and dying life forms in it are thrown out. A few marketable species are retained.

"This is like taking a front-end loader and scraping up your entire front garden and shredding it, keeping a few pebbles, and dumping the rest of it down the drain," says the Spirit. "Couple this with overfishing—really easy to do with megaships equipped with sonar for fast fish finding—and the eventual result is no fish. When smaller boats were still in use, fisheries were sustainable, more or less. But in the past forty years, hyper-efficient hi-tech practices have put paid to a third of the productive ocean. People think it will grow back, and maybe it will, but not for thousands of years. Now you've got bigger and bigger boats chasing smaller and fewer fish. The dumb thing is, the fishing fleets that are causing the most damage are subsidized by their governments, so people aren't paying anything near the cost of the fish they're eating, not directly. But they're paying through their taxes."

"Taxes!" yelps Scrooge. Taxes are a sore spot with him. "You mean, I'm paying for all this effing waste?"

"That's not the only effing waste you're paying for," says the Spirit. "Need I mention the farm policies of certain governments, which subsidize biofuels that cost more energy to produce than the energy that comes back out of them? And the real cost is much higher when you factor in the cost to the land — the soil depletion, and the destruction caused to biosystems by pesticides and herbicides. Then there's the effect on world food prices when you burn food crops instead of eating them — taking biomass out of circulation and replacing it with smoke. With the overfishing, though, help may be at hand: when fuel prices climb too high, those megaships will cost too much to run, especially since they won't have many fish left to, as they say, 'harvest,' the catch per effort having declined 80 percent in thirty years."

Scrooge doesn't feel so good. He can hear his Chilean sea bass dinner reproaching him from inside his stomach.

Next they visit the Amazonian rainforest, which is being mowed down at great speed to allow a few short years of soybean and cattle production; and then the Congo, where deforestation is proceeding at a galloping speed; and then the boreal forests in the north, where trees are being munched up like toothpicks. "A mature tree creates two-thirds of the oxygen a human being needs to breathe," the Spirit comments. "Level millions of trees and make millions of new people every year, and what will happen to the air quality? I won't even mention the floods and soil erosion and subsequent droughts that are the predictable results of cutting trees in the wrong places."

They cruise over the Antarctic, where huge shelves of ice are breaking off and melting, and the Arctic, where the thawing tundra is releasing immense clouds of methane gas. They monitor rising sea levels, and watch while people drown or flee, and check out a couple of superforce cyclones as they zero in on populous low-lying shorelines.

"Can't you stop all this?" Scrooge cries.

"International laws in this area are hard to achieve," says the Spirit, "because no one can agree on what's fair. It's like monkeys: if one has a grape, the others all want grapes. 'You've ruined your own ecology for profit,' say the poorer countries, 'so don't tell us not to do the same.' The killing of the Earth is driven on by poverty on the one hand and greed on the other. Keep in mind also that many of the countries where the most destruction is going on are heavily in debt to the rich ones. So the killing is also driven on by debt.

"The International Monetary Fund and the World Bank — begun in the 1940s to so-called help the so-called developing world — convinced the often-unscrupulous leaders in those countries to borrow lots of money. The leaders were then at liberty to overspend, and to grind their own peasants in order to pay back the ever-accumulating debts. In desperation, the peasants overfarmed the land, which reduced their crop yields and made them even poorer and more subject to famines than they were before. It's a lot like the Roman Empire's tax-farming system: a top-down method of extracting wealth from the poor. The result is what we have today: the incomes of the twenty-five million richest individuals on the planet have a combined net worth that equals the combined net worth of the two billion poorest people on the planet."

Scrooge is about to say that rich people deserve to be rich because of their superior genes and moral fibre, but he catches the Spirit frowning at him and refrains.

"Wouldn't you say," says the Spirit, "that there's a great incentive for people to do what they've done so often before when the imbalance between debt and credit — and poverty and wealth — becomes too great, and the poor find themselves sinking and dying under their crushing debt loads, and the human sense of fairness and justice becomes too outraged? They depose their leaders; or they kill their creditors, if they can get hold of them; or they simply default on their loans."

"But that would screw up the whole system," says Scrooge.

"You miss my point," says the Spirit. "It's already screwed up."

DESCENDING FROM the stratosphere, they find themselves at a dinner party in Toronto. No starving peasants here; the table is loaded with food and drink. Well-dressed people are engaged in friendly converse. The subject is the world food shortage of spring 2008 and the food riots that have quickly resulted.

"It's the food speculators," one guest is saying. "They're hoarding. Do you know how many billions the big corporations have made out of this?"

"No, there really isn't enough food," says a second guest.

"We always can grow more," another says.

"Sure," says the second. "Until we can't. You can't keep taking and taking without putting back."

"The Green Revolution has increased production, what with the fertilizers and pesticides and the genetically modified seeds..." says another.

"Increased it at first," says the second. "Then it burned out, leaving dead soil. The only farmers doing well in the so-called Green Revolution parts of India now are the organic ones."

"What about when all the Chinese and Indians get cars?" says a fourth. "We'll suffocate!"

"Rising gas prices will put a stop to that," says the first. "They won't be able to afford to drive them."

"Too many people," says the second. "Only 20 percent of the earth is dry land. Out of this 20 percent only 3 percent is suitable for crop production. Most of the people on Earth live on 2 percent of the land. We're running out of habitat, and destroying what we have left."

"We've heard these Malthusian predictions before," says the third.

"That doesn't mean they aren't true," says a fourth.

"Well, anyway," says a fifth, "nothing I can do will stop whatever it is that's happening. It's too big for us! We might as well enjoy ourselves while we can." And they all lift their glasses to that.

"Don't be so stupid!" Scrooge barks at them. But they can't hear him. Their merry laughter fades away, and the next moment he's back in the 1972 cellar, the one with the older woman and the steamer trunk. But now it's the present time, and a different older woman is opening the trunk. She finds the envelope left there three or four decades earlier and opens it. "I wonder why Mother saved this," she says to herself.

Scrooge reads over her shoulder. The clipping is from the *Los Angeles Times*. "By 2042, MIT Team Says: Collapse of World Economy Forseen If Growth Goes On," is the header. The story is about a thirteen-month study commissioned by the Club of Rome and conducted by a team of scientists at MIT. "The world economy is headed for collapse within 70 years — bringing widespread pestilence, poverty and starvation — unless economic growth is halted soon," it begins. "The notion that growth of population and material goods cannot go on forever, because there is only a finite supply of land and natural resources on the earth, is hardly new. It is at least as old as Plato." It concludes: "These physical limits to growth are likely to be encountered in the lifetime of our children. The study focuses on five major variables: the world's total non-renewable supply of resources (metal, rock, energy), plus the level of population, the amount of pollution, the rate of industrial output per capita and the amount of food production per capita."

"They knew!" Scrooge yells. "They knew back then in 1972! Why didn't they do something, when there was still time?" In his anger he clutches the Spirit of Earth Day Present by his hemp T-shirt and begins shaking him. But the clock is striking twelve, and under his hands the Spirit is dissolving.

IT'S CHANGING TO something dry and scaly. Now it's a giant cockroach. "I am the Spirit of Earth Day Future," it says in a rasping voice.

Scrooge recoils. He hates bugs. "Can't you look like a human being?" he says.

"That depends on which future you'd like to see," says the cockroach. "In some of the medium-distant futures, humanity will be extinct, and I can hardly take the shape of a bioform that no longer exists."

"How about something closer in time, then?" Scrooge wheedles.

"Okay," says the cockroach. He wavers and dissolves and re-forms: he's a glinty-eyed thirty-five-year-old in a dark suit and a gold earring, carrying a briefcase. "There," he says. "Now I'm a futures trader. Which of your own futures would you like to visit?"

"I've got more than one?" Scrooge asks.

"With futures, it's all probability," says the Spirit. "Futures are infinite in number, as many science-fiction writers have told us. For instance, in one future you've had advanced gene therapy and you live to a hundred and fifty; and in another, you get run over by a bus next week."

"I'll take a pass on that one," says Scrooge hastily.

"It's not all bad," says the Spirit. "In that future you've made a choice for natural burial, so you get reincarnated as a tree. But I see your point. So, the good news or the bad news?"

"The good news first," says Scrooge, who's an optimist about himself, despite being a misanthrope when it comes to everyone else.

The Spirit waves his briefcase, and Scrooge finds himself in a cheerful, bustling medium-sized city. All the people are wearing natural-fibre clothing and riding on bicycles or driving around in compressed-air vehicles and using power from wave-generation machines and from solar installations on the tops and sides of their buildings; everyone has given up junk food and is eating a lot of fruits and vegetables, grown on nearby organic farms or on their erstwhile front lawns, where the top-soil has been restored by an extensive program of mulching and composting — a process that, not inciden-tally, has significantly reduced the carbon dioxide in the air. No one is overweight; all tall buildings turn out their lights during bird migrations, so they're no longer kill-ing millions of birds every year; evil bottom-scraping fishing practices have been abandoned; air travel takes place by helium airship, water travel by solar-controlled sailing ships; plastic shopping bags have been banned.

All religious leaders have realized that their mandate includes helping to preserve the Almighty's gift of the Earth and have condoned birth control; there are no more noisy, polluting gas-powered leaf blowers or lawn mowers; and global warming has been dealt with at a summit during which world leaders gave up paranoia, envy, rivalry, power-hunger, greed, and the debate over who should start cutting down the carbon footprint first, and rolled up their sleeves and got on with it.

There is Scrooge himself, looking very fit in a hemp suit, signing several enormous cheques for conservation organizations: rain-forest stewardship, underwater marine parks, bird habitats. "In this future," says the Spirit, "the albatross has been saved; largely — I must add — through your efforts. I ought to say also that a lot of these miraculous changes have been brought about by a Victory Bond drive, in which people lent to their governments to finance eco-repairs; and through microeconomics, like that already being practised by the Grameen Bank in Bangladesh, whereby mini-amounts are lent at fair interest rates to very poor people to help them start local, small-scale businesses; and also through massive and voluntary debt cancellations on the part of the rich nations, like those of the ancient Israelites, who decreed a jubilee year every fifty years in which all debts became void."

"How probable is this future?" asks Scrooge.

"Not very probable," the Spirit admits. "Or not yet. But many people in your time are busting a gut to make it happen. Unfortunately, there are a lot more people who are actively opposed to any attempts to help clean up the global mess — a mess that in real terms is costing trillions of dollars a year — because they're making too much money out of the situation as it is. Now for the bad news." He waves his briefcase again.

At first Scrooge barely recognizes his future self. He's gaunt and frantic, and pushing a wheelbarrow full of cash. As he watches, his future self tries to exchange this mountain of money for a can of dog food, but it's no deal.

"Spirit! What's happening?" asks Scrooge. This is truly scary.

"You're witnessing a moment of hyperinflation," says the Spirit. "This has happened many times in the history of money. When people lose faith in the value of a currency, you need more and more money to buy anything; and those that have items of real use and value — such as food or fuel — don't want to sell them, because they fear that the money they receive will be worth a lot less the next day. In effect, money simply melts away, like the illusion it always has been. After all, it's a man-made symbol: it exists only if we agree that it does. And if you can't change it back into the real things it's supposed to signify, it's completely worthless."

"But if I can't buy any food, I'll starve!" Scrooge cries.

"That is indeed a probable result," says the Spirit. "Being rich in the conventional sense doesn't help you if there's nothing you can buy. King Midas wished that everything he touched might turn to gold, and he got his wish; but he starved to death, because the food he touched turned to gold as well. In a world in which everything's been changed into money, there's nothing left to eat. Now let's get the bird's-eye view."

What Scrooge sees as they fly above the city is a lot like what he saw in Europe during the Black Death: chaos, mass death, the breakdown of civic order. All five of the erstwhile Mrs. Scrooges are peddling their bodies on the street in exchange for tinned sardines, with varying success. They don't look very good, having achieved the thin-as-a-model figure through no efforts of their own. The Spirit points to three people fighting over a dead cat, which they intend to eat: Scrooge's future self is one of the three. Nor does he manage to obtain any of the cat for himself: he's too weak. The other two kick him, and leave him on the sidewalk, and make off with their meal.

"This is terrible!" Scrooge whimpers. "Spirit — show me no more!"

"The mills of the gods grind slowly, but they grind exceeding small," says the Spirit. "Mankind made a Faustian bargain as soon as he invented his first technologies, including the bow and arrow. It was then that human beings, instead of limiting their birth rate to keep their population in step with natural resources, decided instead to multiply unchecked. Then they increased the food supply to support this growth by manipulating those resources, inventing ever newer and more complex technologies to do so. Now we have the most intricate system of gizmos the world has ever known. Our technological system is the mill that grinds out anything you wish to order up, but no one knows how to turn it off. The end result of a totally efficient technological exploitation of Nature would be a lifeless desert: all natural capital would be exhausted, having been devoured by the mills of production, and the resulting debt to Nature would be infinite. But long before then, payback time will come for Mankind."

Scrooge is terrified, but at the same time he's been making some rapid calculations. If the good future is the real one, he should invest in alternative energies and desalination plants, and he'll make a killing. If the bad future is the real one, he needs to corner the dog food market and build himself a fortified underground bunker, with piped-in oxygen, and he'll end up controlling the world, or what's left of it.

"Men's courses will foreshadow certain ends, to which, if persevered in, they must lead," says Scrooge, quoting his famous forebear. "But if the courses be departed from, the ends will change. Say it is thus with what you show me!"

"I deal in futures," says the Spirit of Earth Day Future. "My best offer is Maybe."

Scrooge clutches the Spirit's arm, which shrinks, collapses, and dwindles down into a bedpost. His own bedpost! "What a horrible dream," he thinks. "But so far, only a dream. I will live in the Past, the Present, and the Future — the Spirits of all three Earth Days shall strive within me! I have time to make amends!"

IN THE NON-FICTIONAL world, in which you and I do something called "existing" and Scrooge does not, we've been discussing various ways of looking at debt. Like all our financial arrangements, and like all our rules of moral conduct — in fact, like language itself — notions about debt form part of the elaborate imaginative construct that is human society. What is true of each part of that mental construct is also true of debt, in all its many variations: because it is a mental construct, how we think about it changes how it works.

Maybe it's time for us to think about it differently. Maybe we need to count things, and add things up, and measure things, in a different way. In fact, maybe we need to count and weigh and measure different things altogether. Maybe we need to calculate the real costs of how we've been living, and of the natural resources we've been taking out of the biosphere. Is this likely to happen? Like the Spirit of Earth Day Future's, my best offer is Maybe.

SCROOGE CLIMBS OUT of his bed and goes to the window. There's the world. It's very beautiful, what with the trees and the sky and so forth. It used to look solid, but now it appears fragile, like a reflection on water: a breath of wind would ripple it, and it would vanish.

I don't really own anything, Scrooge thinks. Not even my body. Everything I have is only borrowed. I'm not really rich at all, I'm heavily in debt. How do I even begin to pay back what I owe? Where should I start?

(NOTES)

As befits the lecture form, this book was written with a listener in mind.

ONE: ANCIENT BALANCES

This chapter is dedicated to the Royal Ontario Museum in Toronto, where my interest in Egyptian coffins was awakened when I was nine; to my father, Dr. C. E. Atwood, through whom I read *The Water Babies*; and to all the children I babysat and watched over at summer camps and in the home — stern teachers in the ways of tit-for-tat.

For the Setons, father and son, see Redekop, Magdalene. *Ernest Thompson Seton*. Toronto: Fitzhenry & Whiteside, 1979.

Tooth fairies and banks: It is in fact true that if you stop believing in banks they will expire.

The statistics on debt are from cbc *Marketplace*: "Debt Nation."

The friend who wrote me the letter about the mortgages was Valerie Martin; I thank her for her permission to use it.

The United Church is the United Church of Canada, formed by a union between the Methodists and some of the Presbyterians.

I came across Frans de Waal's comment on the nature of culture in *Harper's* magazine, June 2008, in an article by Frank Bures called "A Mind Dismembered: In Search of the Magical Penis Thieves."

I thank my brother, neurophysiologist Dr. Harold L. Atwood, for sending me various articles on epigenetics.

There are many variants to the "Punch-buggy, no punch-backs" game. In one, the colour of the Beetle must be specified. I leave it to the experts to dispute the many rules.

For primate trading, see De Waal, Frans, and S. F. Brosnan. "Monkeys Reject Unequal Pay." *Nature* (2003): 425.

Fisher, Daniel. "Selling the Blue Sky." *Forbes.com*. 2008. *Forbes*. 20 February 2008. <http://www.forbes.com/business/global/2008/0310/ 070.html>.

———. "Primate Economics." *Forbes.com*. 2008. Forbes. 22 February 2008. <http://www.forbes.com/2006/02/11/monkey-economics-money_cz_df_money06_0214monkeys.html>.

Surowiecki, James. "The Coup de Grasso." *The New Yorker*. 10 October 2005. Condenet. 28 February 2008. <http://www.newyorker.com/archive/2003/10/06/031006ta_talk_surowiecki>.

Also Wright, Robert. *The Moral Animal: Evolutionary Psychology and Everyday Life*. New York: Vintage, 1994. The 1995 reprint is subtitled "Why We Are the Way We Are." Pages 196, 197, 198, 204.

There are probably some other reasons for the femaleness of Charles Kingsley's Bedoneby twins; for these, see my introductions to Rider Haggard's *She*, New American Library, and H. G. Wells's

The Island of Doctor Moreau, Penguin, as well as my unfinished
thesis on supernatural Victorian female characters, which is
somewhere in the Fisher Library of the University of Toronto.

There is much work on the relationship between Kingsley and
Darwin. But see primarily the reverse-evolution fable within the
novel, in which human beings revert to a primitive state by lying
under the flapdoodle trees and effortlessly eating flapdoodle.

The story of Dives and Lazarus is in Luke 16:19–31.

For gelada monkeys, see Morell, Virginia. "Kings of the Hill."
National Geographic.com. 2002. National Geographic Society. 20
February 2008. <http://ngm.nationalgeographic.com/ngm/0211/
feature4/>.

Quotes from *The Eumenides* are from Grene, David, and Richmond
Lattimore, eds. *The Complete Greek Tragedies*. Vol. 1. Chicago:
University of Chicago Press, 1960.

For ancient gods and goddesses, see, among others, "Thoth, the
Great God of Science and Writing." *Mystae.com*. 24 February 2008.
<http://www.mystae.com/restricted/streams/scripts/thoth.html>.

Hooker, Richard. "Ma'at: Goddess of Truth; Truth and Order." *World
Civilizations*. 1996. Washington State University. 24 February 2008.
<http://www.wsu.edu:8080/~dee/egypt/maat.htm>.

Roe, Anthony. "Maintaining the Balance: Concepts of Cosmic
Law, Order, and Justice." *White Dragon*. 1998. 22 February 2008.
<http://www.whitedragon.org.uk/articles/cosmic.htm>.

Swatt, Barbara. "Themis, God of Justice." *Marian Gould
Gallagher Law Library*. 2007. University of Washington School of
Law. 19 February 2008. <http://lib.law.washington.edu/ref/
themis.html>.

TWO: DEBT AND SIN

This chapter is dedicated to Aileen Christianson of Scotland, to Valerie Martin of the United States, and to Alice Munro of Canada — experts on sin and debt, all. Also to my mother, Margaret K. Atwood, and to my aunt, Joyce Barkhouse, for the insights they have provided on living within your means.

The person who said, "Debt is the new fat," was Judith Timson, in a conversation with me.

The Anglican Church of Canada is quite a lot like the Anglican Church of England, and somewhat like the Episcopalian Church in the United States.

Joyce Barkhouse thinks my father got his pawnable pen from his mother as a graduation gift. Which raises another question: How could she have afforded it, since she didn't have a bean either? She must have saved up for a long time.

The word "redeem" is also repeatedly used in the Jewish seder ceremony to describe what God did in reference to the Israelites when he freed them from slavery in Egypt. I thank Rosalie and Irving Abella for this knowledge, and for a seder experience that will never be forgotten.

Redeeming a donkey with a lamb may be found in Exodus 34:20. The story of Jephthah's daughter is in Kings 1. The first-born belonging to God is in Exodus 22:29. The wicked borrowing and paying not again is in Psalms 37:21. Elijah and the priests of Baal are in Kings 1.

The sermon on debt is to be found at Olbrych, Jennie C. "Outrageous Forgiveness." *St. James Santee Episcopal Church Blog*. 2004. Blogspot. 12 March 2008. <http://stjamessantee.blogspot.com/2004_09_01_archive.html>.

Other works cited include

Hogg, James. *The Private Memoirs and Confessions of a Justified Sinner.* Ed. Adrian Hunter. Peterborough, Ontario: Broadview Press, 2001.

Hyde, Lewis. *The Gift: How the Creative Spirit Transforms the World.* 1983. Edinburgh: Canongate, 2007. Page 41.

Jacobs, Jane. *Systems of Survival: A Dialogue on the Moral Foundations of Commerce and Politics.* New York: Vintage, 1992.

Leith, Sam. "Blair Believes He Can Do No Wrong: Ask the Antinomians." *Telegraph.co.uk.* 2006. Telegraph Media Group. 2 March 2008. <http://www.telegraph.co.uk/opinion/main.jhtml?xml=/opinion/2006/03/25/do2504.xml>.

Lerner, Gerda. *The Creation of Patriarchy.* Uncorrected proof. New York: Oxford University Press, 1986. Pages 77, 84.

Milton, John. "Samson Agonistes." *John Milton: Selections.* Ed. Stephen Orgel and Jonathan Goldberg. Oxford: Oxford University Press, 1991.

———. "Paradise Lost." *John Milton: Selections.* Ed. Stephen Orgel and Jonathan Goldberg. Oxford: Oxford University Press, 1991.

Orwell, George. *1984.* New York: Harcourt, 1983. Page 256.

Tierney, Patrick. *The Highest Altar: The Story of Human Sacrifice.* New York: Viking, 1989. Page 277.

Webb, Mary. *Precious Bane.* Notre Dame, Indiana: University of Notre Dame Press, 2003. Page 43.

Zola, Émile. *Germinal.* Trans. Peter Collier. Oxford: Oxford University Press, 1993.

THREE: DEBT AS PLOT

This chapter is dedicated to Miss Bessie B. Billings and Miss Florence Smedley, my English teachers at Leaside High School in Toronto, where I first read *The Mill on the Floss*; to Dr. Jay Macpherson of Victoria College, who made the Victorian novel a thing of splendour and intrigue; and to Dr. Jerome H. Buckley of the

Harvard English Department, who did some very dramatic readings of Dickens. Also to the Deer Park Library in Toronto, from which, in the late 1940s, I borrowed every Andrew Lang fairy book I could get my hands on.

The books used or cited in this chapter are

Berne, Eric. *Games People Play: The Psychology of Human Relationships*. New York: Ballantine, 1964. Page 81.

Blake, William. "Jerusalem." *Selected Poetry and Prose*. Ed. Northrop Frye. New York: Random House, 1953.

Bunyan, John. *The Pilgrim's Progress*. Ed. Roger Sharrock. New York: Penguin, 1987. Page 79.

Dickens, Charles. *A Christmas Carol*. New York: Weathervane, 2007.

Eliot, George. *The Mill on the Floss*. Ed. Gordon S. Haight. New York: Oxford University Press, 1996. Page 252, 356, 359.

Hardy, Thomas. "The Ruined Maid." *Complete Poems*. Ed. James Gibson. New York: Palgrave, 2001.

Irving, Washington. "The Devil and Tom Walker." Internet text version.

Lang, Andrew. *The Blue Fairy Book*. New York: Dover, 1965.

Marlowe, Christopher. *The Tragical History of Doctor Faustus*. Ed. David Scott Kastan. New York: Norton, 2005.

Thackeray, W. M. *Vanity Fair*. 1908. Ed. Whitelaw Reid. London: Aldine Press, 1957.

The texts of quotations from Chaucer are standard.

Grimm's Fairy Tales were read by me at an early age, and remembered well.

Valerie Martin drew my attention to the game of Forfeits.

A note on "redeem": "To redeem" is thus also to rename — or redefine — yourself, which can lead to reversing the doom.

"The Miller of Dee" came from memory, but I also checked it against available texts.

CHAPTER FOUR: THE SHADOW SIDE

This chapter is dedicated to Edgar Allan Poe, whose story "The Cask of Amontillado" terrified me as a child reader, and set me to thinking about the ever-present question: how much revenge is enough? Also to Alberto Manguel, who once said to me, "Canadians don't have any revenge stories," thus prompting me to write one: "Hairball," it is called. And to Elmore Leonard, charming explicator of the ways of the underside. And to Larry Gaynor, who knows what shadows lurk in the hearts of men, and also what hearts lurk in the shadows of women.

Another real-life revenge is the frozen shrimp in the curtain rods. So easy to smell, so hard to find.

Works cited include

Buchan, James. *Frozen Desire: The Meaning of Money*. New York: Welcome Rain, 2001.

Dickens, Charles. *A Tale of Two Cities*. Ed. Andrew Sanders. Oxford: Oxford University Press, 1988.

———. *David Copperfield*. Ed. Nina Burgis. Oxford: Oxford University Press, 1999.

Johnson, Samuel. *Essays from the Rambler, Adventurer, and Idler*. Ed. W. J. Bate. New Haven: Yale University Press, 1968.

Leonard, Elmore. *Get Shorty*. New York: HarperCollins, 1990. Page 8.

Machiavelli, Niccolò. *The Prince*. Trans. Peter Constantine. New York: Random House, 2007.

Shakespeare, William. "The Merchant of Venice." *Complete Works*. Ed. Richard Proudfoot, Ann Thompson, and David Scott Kastan. London: Arden Shakespeare, 2001.

FIVE: PAYBACK

There are so many people and organizations to whom this chapter might be dedicated that it was hard to choose. So I'll single out my instructors on the subject of traditional life in the Arctic — Aaju Peter,

Bernadette Dean, and John Houston — and also Matthew Swan of Adventure Canada, who made such contacts possible. And Graeme Gibson, whose work on predators and their prey and their environments has overlapped with mine.

Belshazzar's feast may be found in Daniel 5.

John Donne's bell comment is in the *Devotions*, "Meditation xvii."

I posit that Scrooge Nouveau's inherited fortune would have come through Scrooge's happy nephew, Fred, son of his dead sister, Fan — thus Scrooge's closest relative. Scrooge Lite left a lot of his money to charity, but Fred got the business and took the surname Scrooge to preserve it in the family firm.

Scrooge Nouveau's CEO, Bob Cratchit, is a descendant of the original Bob, via Tiny Tim. Not being athletic, Tim took to the books and became a proto-nerd; Scrooge Lite funded his education. The new Bob has, however, few of the virtues of the original one.

For "feeding the earth," see Patrick Tierney's *The Highest Altar*, previously cited.

There is much information on Solon and his debt reforms, but see for instance John Ralston Saul's *Voltaire's Bastards*.

There are many books on the Black Death. But see, for instance, Duncan, Christopher, and Susan Scott. *Return of the Black Death: The World's Greatest Serial Killer.* Chichester: Wiley, 2004. And also Kelly, John. *The Great Mortality: An Intimate History of the Black Death, the Most Devastating Plague of All Time.* Toronto: HarperCollins, 2005.

The Blake quotation is from the poem "The Human Abstract."

The sixty-three-year-old woman who put the newspaper clipping into the steamer trunk was my mother. She'd cut it out of the *Toronto*

Star, which had reprinted it from the *Los Angeles Times*. The person who found it and read it much later — in 2008 — was me.

For the Spirit of Earth Day Present's coffee choice, see Bridget Stutchbury, *The Silence of the Songbirds*.

There is a great deal of material on the destruction of the ocean. See, for instance, Jones, Deborah. "In a Few Decades, There Will Be No Fish." *globeandmail.com*. 2005. *Globe and Mail*. 21 May 2008. <http://www.theglobeandmail.com/servlet/Page/document/v5/content/>.

For good fish choices, consult www.seafoodwatch.org. For how to help, see www.Oceana.org.

The statistic on the oxygen production of trees comes from www.torontoparksandtrees.org.

For the beneficial effects of organic soil on carbon dioxide, see Beck, Malcolm. *The Secret Life of Compost*. Metairie, Louisiana: Acres, 1997. See also www.FarmForward.com.

For birds killed by lighted buildings and for what you can do to help, see, for instance, FLAP, at www.flap.org. There are many other organizations working on this, and on the bird/windfarm interaction. If you are a city official or a corporate high-rise renter, why not turn off the lights, save some carbons, and stop murdering migrating birds at the same time? How hard is that, actually?

To help save the albatross from extinction, go to the BirdLife International website at www.birdlife.org, find the BirdLife partner organization in your own country, and contribute to it.

For helping to save the migratory songbirds, see not only BirdLife International, but also the American Bird Conservancy, at www.abcbirds.org.

The Grameen Bank is just one example of microfinancing.

For hyperinflation moments, see, for instance, Buchan, James. *Frozen Desire: The Meaning of Money*. New York: Welcome Rain, 2001.

For the relentless destructiveness of certain kinds of technologies, see Juenger, Friedrich George. *The Failure of Technology: Perfection Without Purpose*. Hinsdale, Illinois: Henry Regnery, 1949.

Scrooge's bad future might prove to be even worse. For a prophet of the tipping point, see James Lovelock's *The Revenge of Gaia*. London: Allen Lane, 2006.

For examples of earlier and more inclusive attitudes toward animals, read the story of Noah, carefully; see the life of Buddha; consult Hinduism and vegetarianism; and see too the charming Muslim fable *The Animals' Lawsuit Against Humanity*, as well as the strictures against the abuse of animals in the Koran. I thank Dr. Tazim Kassan of Syracuse University for bringing these last to my attention.

Some of the ingested biofuel that kept this author at the keyboard came from fair-trade, organic, shade-grown chocolate bars, the only kind that are bird-friendly.

Carbon-neutral electric energy was supplied by Bullfrog Power at www.bullfrogpower.com.

It is worth mentioning that a ridiculously low 1.5 percent of all charitable giving goes to non-human Nature, excluding pets. That statistic can be changed by you.

A sum equalling the author's net profit from the Canadian advance for this book has been donated to BirdLife International, through its partner, Nature Canada.

(BIBLIOGRAPHY)

"The Animals' Lawsuit Against Humanity." *Fons Vitae Book Catalogue*. 2008. Fons Vitae. 28 May 2008. <http://www.fonsvitae.com/animalslawsuit.html>.

Beck, Malcolm. *The Secret Life of Compost*. Metairie, Louisiana: Acres, 1997.

Beckett, Samuel. *Waiting for Godot*. Ed. Dougald McMillan and James Knowlson. London: Faber, 1993.

Berne, Eric. *Games People Play: The Psychology of Human Relationships*. New York: Ballantine, 1964.

Blake, William. "Jerusalem." "The Human Abstract." *Selected Poetry and Prose*. Ed. Northrop Frye. New York: Random House, 1953.

Buchan, James. *Frozen Desire: The Meaning of Money*. New York: Welcome Rain, 2001.

Bunyan, John. *The Pilgrim's Progress*. Ed. Roger Sharrock. New York: Penguin, 1987.

Burns, Robert. "The Deil's Awa' wi' the Exciseman." *Poems, Songs, and Letters: The Complete Works of Robert Burns*. Ed. Alexander Smith. London: Macmillan, 1932.

Chapman, Sasha. "Wanted: Organic Farmers to Fill Toronto's Markets." *Globe and Mail*. 24 May 2008: M5.

Cooper, James Fenimore. *The Pioneers*. New York: Grosset and Dunlap, 1948.

De Waal, Frans, and S. F. Brosnan. "Monkeys Reject Unequal Pay."
    Nature (2003): 425.
Dickens, Charles. *A Christmas Carol*. New York: Weathervane, 2007.
———. *David Copperfield*. Ed. Nina Burgis. Oxford: Oxford
    University Press, 1999.
———. *A Tale of Two Cities*. Ed. Andrew Sanders. Oxford: Oxford
    University Press, 1988.
Duncan, Christopher, and Susan Scott. *Return of the Black Death:
    The World's Greatest Serial Killer*. Chichester: Wiley, 2004.
Eliot, George. *The Mill on the Floss*. Ed. Gordon S. Haight. New York:
    Oxford University Press, 1996.
"The Figure of Saint Michael Archangel." *Saint Michael the Shrine on
    the Gargano*. 1998–99. Asernet. 22 February 2008. <http://www.
    gargano.it/sanmichele/english/santo1_en.htm>.
Fisher, Daniel. "Selling the Blue Sky." *Forbes.com*. 20 February 2008.
    <http://www.forbes.com/business/global/2008/0310/070.html>.
———. "Primate Economics." *Forbes.com*. 2008. 22 February 2008.
    <http://www.forbes.com/2006/02/11/monkey-economics-
    money_cz_df_money06_0214monkeys.html>.
Freud, Sigmund. *The Standard Edition of the Complete Psychological
    Works of Sigmund Freud*. Ed. James Strachey. 24 vols. London:
    Vintage, 2001.
Goodman, Amy. "Ticker Tape Ain't Spaghetti." 30 April 2008.
    Truthdig. 2 May 2008. <www.truthdig.com/report/
    item/20080430_ticker_tape_aint_spaghetti>.
"Grameen Bank." *Grameen Bank*. 1998. Grameen Communications.
    5 May 2008. <http://www.grameen-info.org/>.
Grene, David, and Richmond Lattimore, eds. *The Complete Greek
    Tragedies*. Vol. 1. Chicago: University of Chicago Press, 1960.
Hardy, Thomas. "The Ruined Maid." *Complete Poems*. Ed. James
    Gibson. New York: Palgrave, 2001.
Hogg, James. *The Private Memoirs and Confessions of a Justified
    Sinner*. Ed. Adrian Hunter. Peterborough, Ontario: Broadview
    Press, 2001.
Hooker, Richard. "Ma'at: Goddess of Truth; Truth and Order." *World
    Civilizations*. 1996. Washington State University. 24 February
    2008. <http://www.wsu.edu:8080/~dee/egypt/maat.htm>

Hurdle, John. "Where Industry Once Hummed, Urban Garden Finds Success." *New York Times*. 20 May 2008.

Hyde, Lewis. *The Gift: How the Creative Spirit Transforms the World*. Edinburgh: Canongate, 2007.

Jacobs, Jane. *Systems of Survival: A Dialogue on the Moral Foundations of Commerce and Politics*. New York: Vintage, 1992.

Johnson, Samuel. *Essays from the Rambler, Adventurer, and Idler*. Ed. W. J. Bate. New Haven: Yale University Press, 1968.

Jones, Deborah. "In a Few Decades, There Will Be No Fish." *globeandmail.com*. 2005. *Globe and Mail*. 21 May 2008. <http://www.theglobeandmail.com/servlet/Page/document/v5/content/>.

Juenger, Friedrich George. *The Failure of Technology: Perfection Without Purpose*. Hinsdale, Illinois: Henry Regnery, 1949.

Jung, C. G. *Psychology and Religion*. New Haven: Yale University Press, 1992.

Kelly, John. *The Great Mortality: An Intimate History of the Black Death, the Most Devastating Plague of All Time*. Toronto: HarperCollins, 2005.

Kingsley, Charles. *The Water Babies*. Ed. Brian Anderson. Oxford: Oxford University Press, 2000.

Kohler, Nicholas. "A Nation of Eco-Hogs." *Maclean's*. 28 April 2008.

Lang, Andrew. *The Blue Fairy Book*. New York: Dover, 1965.

Lean, Geoffrey. "Exposed: The Great GM Crops Myth." *independent.co.uk*. 20 April 2008. <www.independent.co.uk/environment/greenliving/exposed-the-great-gm-crops-myth-812179.html>.

Leith, Sam. "Blair Believes He Can Do No Wrong: Ask the Antinomians." *telegraph.co.uk*. 2006. Telegraph Media Group. 2 March 2008. <http://www.telegraph.co.uk/opinion/main.jhtml?xml=/opinion/ 2006/03/25/do2504.xml>.

Leonard, Elmore. *Get Shorty*. New York: HarperCollins, 1990.

Lerner, Gerda. *The Creation of Patriarchy*. Uncorrected proof. New York: Oxford University Press, 1986.

Lovelock, James. *The Revenge of Gaia*. London: Allen Lane, 2006.

Machiavelli, Niccolò. *The Prince*. Trans. Peter Constantine. New York: Random House, 2007.

Marlowe, Christopher. *The Tragical History of Doctor Faustus*. Ed. David Scott Kastan. New York: Norton, 2005.

McCarthy, Michael. "The Great Migration Crisis." *Commondreams. org.* 2008. News Center. 1 May 2008. <http://www.common-dreams.org/archive/2008/04/21/8419/>.

McNeill, William H. *Plagues and Peoples.* New York: Doubleday, 1976.

Milton, John. "Paradise Lost." *John Milton: Selections.* Ed. Stephen Orgel and Jonathan Goldberg. Oxford: Oxford University Press, 1991.

———. "Samson Agonistes." *John Milton: Selections.* Ed. Stephen Orgel and Jonathan Goldberg. Oxford: Oxford University Press, 1991.

Morell, Virginia. "Kings of the Hill." *National Geographic.com.* 2002. National Geographic Society. 20 February 2008. <http://ngm. nationalgeographic.com/ngm/0211/feature4/>.

O'Connell, Stephen A. "Debt Forgiveness: Plainer Speaking, Please." *Swarthmore College.* 2000. 28 March 2008. <www.swarthmore. edu/SocSci/soconne1/documents/forgive.pdf>.

Olbrych, Jennie C. "Outrageous Forgiveness." *St. James Santee Episcopal Church Blog.* 2004. Blogspot. 12 March 2008. <http:// stjamessantee.blogspot.com/2004_09_01_archive.html>.

Orwell, George. *1984.* New York: Harcourt, 1983.

"Owed Justice: Thai Women Trafficked into Debt Bondage in Japan." *Human Rights Watch.* 2000. Human Rights Watch. 3 April 2008. <http://www.hrw.org/reports/2000/japan/>.

Polanyi, Karl. *The Great Transformation.* Boston: Beacon Press, 1957.

Redekop, Magdalene. *Ernest Thompson Seton.* Toronto: Fitzhenry & Whiteside, 1979.

Roe, Anthony. "Maintaining the Balance: Concepts of Cosmic Law, Order, and Justice." *White Dragon.* 1998. 22 February 2008. <http://www.whitedragon.org.uk/articles/cosmic.htm>.

Saul, John Ralston. *Voltaire's Bastards: The Dictatorship of Reason in the West.* New York: Vintage, 1993.

Scott, James C. "Revolution in the Revolution: Peasants and Commissars." *Theory and Society* 7 (1979): 117.

Shakespeare, William. "Hamlet." *Complete Works.* Ed. Richard Proudfoot, Ann Thompson, and David Scott Kastan. London: Arden Shakespeare, 2001.

———. "Macbeth."*Complete Works.* Ed. Richard Proudfoot, Ann Thompson, and David Scott Kastan. London: Arden Shakespeare, 2001.

————. "The Merchant of Venice." *Complete Works*. Ed. Richard Proudfoot, Ann Thompson, and David Scott Kastan. London: Arden Shakespeare, 2001.

"The Small Hands of Slavery: Bonded Child Labour in India." *Human Rights Watch*. 1996. Human Rights Watch. 4 April 2008. < http://www.hrw.org/reports/1996/India3.htm>.

Steiger, Paul. "By 2042, MIT Team Says: Collapse of World Economy Foreseen If Growth Goes On." *Los Angeles Times*. 3 March 1972.

Surowiecki, James. "The Coup de Grasso." *The New Yorker*. 10 October 2005. Condenet. 28 February 2008. <http://www.newyorker.com/archive/2003/10/06/031006ta_talk_surowiecki>.

Swatt, Barbara. "Themis, God of Justice." *Marian Gould Gallagher Law Library*. 2007. University of Washington School of Law. 19 February 2008. <http://lib.law.washington.edu/ref/themis.html>.

Thackeray, W. M. *Vanity Fair*. 1908. Ed. Whitelaw Reid. London: Aldine Press, 1957.

"Thoth, the Great God of Science and Writing." *Mystae.com*. 24 February 2008. <http://www.mystae.com/restricted/streams/scripts/thoth.html>.

Tierney, Patrick. *The Highest Altar: The Story of Human Sacrifice*. New York: Viking, 1989.

Traynor, Ian. "Europe Expects a Flood of Climate Refugees." *Guardian Weekly*. 14–20 March 2008: 1.

Ward, Olivia. "$3 Trillion Is Just a Part of the Cost." *Toronto Star*. 16 March 2008: A15.

Webb, Mary. *Precious Bane*. Notre Dame, Indiana: University of Notre Dame Press, 2003.

"The Wheat Sheet: A New Era of Papermaking in Canada." Advertisement. *Markets Initiative*. 15 May 2008.

"Wildife Populations 'Plummeting.'" *BBC News*. 16 May 2008. <http://newsvote.bbc.co.uk/2/hi/uk_news/7403989.stm>.

Wright, Robert. *The Moral Animal: Evolutionary Psychology and Everyday Life*. New York: Vintage, 1994.

Zola, Émile. *Germinal*. Trans. Peter Collier. Oxford: Oxford University Press, 1993.

(ACKNOWLEDGEMENTS)

This project has been a labour of love. I did it for Anansi, and for its proprietor, Scott Griffin, in particular: valour in the face of such daunting challenges as literary publishing in Canada should not go unrewarded, although it usually does.

There are many others to thank. First, my agents, Phoebe Larmore of North America and Vivienne Schuster and Betsy Robbins of the United Kingdom. From House of Anansi Press, Sarah MacLachlan and Lynn Henry. From Bloomsbury, Alexandra Pringle. Heather Sangster, tireless copyeditor. From the CBC, Philip Coulter and Bernie Lucht. From Massey College, Master John Fraser, and the two research assistants he so ably provided in the time of need, Claire Battershill and Dylan Smith.

Thanks to my very helpful first readers, Jess Atwood Gibson and Valerie Martin, and also to Drs. Ramsay and Eleanor Cook, who rightly scribbled "This is silly" in some of the margins. I hope I have managed to take those bits out, though other silly things unnoticed by them may remain. Thanks also to sounding boards David Young and Judith Timson, to whom I blathered on. Thanks also to the O. W. Toad office support staff, Sarah Webster, Shannon Shields, Laura Stenberg, Penny Kavanaugh, and Anne Joldersma, who, when things were falling apart, kept them from falling apart completely.

And finally, thanks to Graeme Gibson, who understands balances and puts up with imbalances, including mine when I'm writing books.

To all, I stand indebted.

(PERMISSIONS)

(THE CBC MASSEY LECTURES SERIES)